WORLD BANK STAFF OCCASIONAL PAPERS □ NUMBER TWENTY-EIGHT

James E. Austin

Confronting
Urban Malnutrition

THE DESIGN OF NUTRITION PROGRAMS

Published for the World Bank
The Johns Hopkins University Press
Baltimore and London

The views and interpretations in this book are those
of the author and should not be attributed to
the World Bank, to its affiliated organizations, or
to any individual acting in their behalf.

Library of Congress Cataloging in Publication Data
Austin, James E
    Confronting urban malnutrition.

    (World Bank staff occasional paper; no. 28)
    Includes bibliographical references.
    1. Food relief. 2. Malnutrition. 3. Food
supply. 4. Urbanization. I. Title. II. Series.
HV696.F6A93   362.5   79-3705
ISBN 0-8018-2261-0

Foreword

I would like to explain why the World Bank does research work and why this research is published. We feel an obligation to look beyond the projects that we help finance toward the whole resource allocation of an economy and the effectiveness of the use of those resources. Our major concern, in dealings with member countries, is that all scarce resources—including capital, skilled labor, enterprise, and know-how—should be used to their best advantage. We want to see policies that encourage appropriate increases in the supply of savings, whether domestic or international. Finally, we are required by our Articles, as well as by inclination, to use objective economic criteria in all our judgments.

These are our preoccupations, and these, one way or another, are the subjects of most of our research work. Clearly, they are also the proper concern of anyone who is interested in promoting development, and so we seek to make our research papers widely available. In doing so, we have to take the risk of being misunderstood. Although these studies are published by the Bank, the views expressed and the methods explored should not necessarily be considered to represent the Bank's views or policies. Rather, they are offered as a modest contribution to the great discussion on how to advance the economic development of the underdeveloped world.

ROBERT S. MCNAMARA
President
The World Bank

Contents

Preface

This book presents an excellent survey of different policies for addressing urban malnutrition. Drawing upon an earlier study completed under his direction, the author presents here a framework that governments and development agencies will find useful for defining the problem and evaluating alternative solutions. Recent experience indicates that malnutrition is a far-from-marginal problem in even the affluent developing countries. Studies by the Food and Agricultural Organization of the United Nations show an increase over the last decade in the number of people whose diets fall below standards required for minimally productive lives. This is certainly unacceptable, particularly for the largely urban, middle- and upper-income developing countries that have the resources to confront the problem.

It is impossible to separate nutrition in cities from that in rural areas, where most of the malnourished live and where food is grown. Many governments have subsidized urban consumers at the expense of rural sectors, which are dominated by small farmers and the landless, themselves often malnourished. Undercapitalized farming, particularly smallholder farming, has led to a situation today in which almost half of all food consumed by people in the developing world's cities must be imported.

The alleviation of urban malnutrition will not be by supplemental feeding schemes or other related programs alone. Raising productivity in rural areas, so that food supplies and incomes both increase, would help reduce urban poverty by generating more abundant food and by mitigating the forces that push labor from the countryside into already overcrowded urban centers. Such increases must be explicit governmental priorities. In addition, the food sector must be managed to provide adequate, equitable incentives for increased production by farmers without adversely affecting consumption by low-income groups. Despite recent shifts in priorities, few governments have been willing to face directly the policy implications of trying to resolve these objectives by effective or consistent interventions in the food sector. This book is a valuable contribution to the examination of one aspect of this multifaceted problem.

MONTAGUE YUDELMAN
Director
Agriculture and Rural Development Department
The World Bank

Acknowledgments

I would like to express my deep appreciation to the following colleagues who collaborated in the preparation of the larger report to the World Bank, "Urban Malnutrition: Problem Assessment and Intervention Guidelines," from which this monograph was derived: John Briscoe, C. K. Chan, John Dixon, Johanna Dwyer, Stanley Gershoff, John Harris, D. Mark Hegsted, M. Guillermo Herrera, Eileen Kennedy, F. J. Levinson, Judith McGuire, Henry Nieder, Barbara Millen Posner, Gordon Rausser, Bea Rogers, Robert Stickney, Flavio Valente, Dave Wheeler, Joe Wray, and Marian Zeitlin.

They demonstrated an exceptional capacity to share—generously, constructively, and patiently—their different disciplinary skills and perspectives. The resultant integration enriched our understanding, and it is our mutual hope that this document will provide greater insights for others as well.

I am also indebted to the following World Bank staff who provided critical and perceptive guidance during the development of this study: Samir Basta, Alan Berg, James Greene, Shlomo Reutlinger, Emmerich Schebeck, Marcelo Selowsky, and Neil Wilkie.

Final thanks go to those who aided the progress of this study into print. Christopher Corkery, David Wray, and Marian Zeitlin gave considerate and thorough editorial assistance to the original report. Beverly Vidler carefully and cheerfully typed the manuscript's many drafts. David Driscoll edited the final manuscript for publication. Proofs of the text and tables were corrected by Chris Jerome through the Word Guild, and the chart was prepared by Raphael Blow of the World Bank's Art and Design Section. James McEuen assisted in completing citations of some of the study's sources and managed production of the book.

Confronting Urban Malnutrition

THE DESIGN OF NUTRITION PROGRAMS

1

Urban Malnutrition: An Introduction

In the tide of change that will engulf the developing countries before the end of the twentieth century, the most dramatic and fundamental force is urbanization. In 1950, 16 percent of the population of developing countries were city dwellers; by the year 2000, 43 percent will inhabit urban areas.[1] No less striking than the absolute increase is the tempo of change: the growth in urban population from 504 million in 1970 to 2.2 billion thirty years later represents a fourfold increase (see Figure 1). Although significant regional variations exist (Table 1-1), intense urbanization is the rule throughout the developing world. Thus, the developing nations must come to terms with urbanization on a vaster scale and within a shorter time than the developed countries had to face.

The effect of this urban explosion is dramatically manifested in teeming slums in the center of the city and mushrooming shanty towns on its periphery. These urban poverty pockets and rings are especially prevalent in large "million plus" cities. Seventy-nine such urban agglomerations existed in developing countries in 1970 with 147 projected for 1985 when they will comprise 38 percent of the total urban population (Table 1-2).

In most of these cities one-fourth to one-half of the population live in intense deprivation and denial of their basic needs.[2] Malnutrition is simultaneously an especially severe contributor to, and consequence of, the urban poverty syndrome. The urban poor suf-

1. United Nations, *Urban and Rural Population* (New York, 1970), Table 5, pp. 14–19.
2. Callisto Eneas Madavo, "Uncontrolled Settlements," *Finance and Development*, vol. 13, no. 1 (March 1976), p. 16; Edward Jaycox, "The Bank and Urban Poverty," *Finance and Development*, vol. 15, no. 3 (September 1978), pp. 10–13.

Figure 1. *Urban Population Growth, 1950–2000*

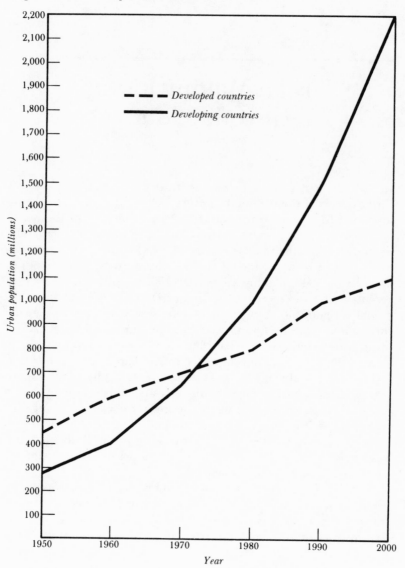

Source: Derived from United Nations, *Urban and Rural Population* (New York, 1970), pp. 14–19.

Table 1-1. *Estimates of Urban, Rural, and Total Population, 1960, 1980, and 2000* (population in millions)

Area	1960				1980				2000			
	Urban	Rural	Total	Percentage urban[a]	Urban	Rural	Total	Percentage urban	Urban	Rural	Total	Percentage urban
World	985	1,997	2,982	33.0	1,854	2,614	4,467	41.5	3,329	3,186	6,515	51.1
More developed	582	394	976	59.6	864	347	1,210	71.4	1,174	280	1,454	80.7
Less developed	403	1,603	2,005	20.1	990	2,267	3,257	30.4	2,155	2,906	5,061	42.6
Asia	333	1,312	1,645	20.2	757	1,824	2,581	29.3	1,515	2,254	3,779	40.1
East	179	601	780	22.9	387	708	1,095	35.3	722	703	1,425	50.7
South	154	711	865	17.8	370	1,116	1,486	24.9	793	1,561	2,354	33.7
Africa	48	222	270	17.9	125	332	457	27.3	320	498	818	39.2
Western	12	68	80	15.3	34	99	133	25.7	96	144	240	39.9
Eastern	6	71	77	7.3	16	113	129	12.7	50	183	233	21.2
Middle	3	26	29	11.5	11	35	46	23.0	33	47	80	40.7
Northern	20	45	65	29.9	49	70	119	40.9	113	101	214	52.9
Southern	8	10	18	41.7	15	14	29	51.7	29	21	50	57.9
Latin America	103	110	213	48.4	238	139	377	63.2	495	157	652	75.9
Tropical	51	61	112	46.0	131	73	204	64.8	296	72	348	79.7
Temperate	23	10	33	69.3	38	9	47	80.5	56	7	63	88.3
Middle	22	26	48	44.9	55	40	95	57.6	125	55	180	69.4
Caribbean	7	14	21	36.1	15	17	32	46.2	28	22	50	56.5

Source: United Nations, *Urban and Rural Population* (New York, 1970), Table 5, pp. 14–19.

a. Percentages are based on unrounded figures and therefore may be different from those which the reader may calculate using the statistics in this table.

5

Table 1-2. *Estimated Number and Population of Million-plus Cities and Percentage of Total and Urban Population Residing in These Cities, 1960, 1980, and 1985* (population in millions)

Area	1960				1980				1985			
	Number of cities	Population	Percent of total population	Percent of urban population	Number of cities	Population	Percent of total population	Percent of urban population	Number of cities	Population	Percent of total population	Percent of urban population
World	109	271	9.1	27.5	229	646	14.5	34.8	273	805	16.3	37.1
More developed	64	173	17.7	29.7	108	294	24.3	34.0	126	340	26.7	36.1
Less developed	45	99	4.9	24.6	121	352	10.8	35.6	147	465	12.7	37.9
Asia	39	92	5.6	27.6	90	281	10.9	37.1	107	361	14.4	37.7
East	23	60	7.7	33.5	50	162	14.8	41.9	54	195	17.0	39.3
South	16	32	3.7	20.8	40	119	8.0	32.2	53	166	10.7	35.6
Africa	3	6	2.2	12.5	14	32	7.0	25.6	19	47	9.1	29.3
Western	—	—	—	—	2	4	3.0	11.8	5	9	6.3	18.1
Eastern	—	—	—	—	2	3	2.3	18.7	3	5	3.1	28.7
Middle	—	—	—	—	1	2	4.3	18.2	1	3	6.4	23.6
Northern	2	5	7.7	25.0	5	17	14.3	34.7	6	22	16.5	36.4
Southern	1	1	5.6	12.5	4	6	20.7	40.0	4	7	21.8	41.3
Latin America	11	31	14.5	30.1	26	94	24.9	39.5	31	121	28.0	42.1
Tropical	6	15	13.4	29.4	16	55	27.0	42.0	20	73	30.5	43.7
Temperate	3	10	30.3	43.5	3	16	34.0	42.1	4	19	40.2	47.2
Middle	1	5	10.4	22.7	4	19	20.0	34.5	4	24	21.7	34.8
Caribbean	1	2	9.5	28.6	3	5	15.6	33.3	3	6	16.6	32.3

Sources: Estimated numbers of cities from United Nations, *The World's Million-plus Cities, 1950–1985* (New York, 1972), Table 1, p. 13. Estimated population, ibid., Table 2, p. 14. Percentages calculated from data in Tables 2 and 3.

fering from caloric deficits are estimated between 200 and 360 million and may reach 260 to 910 million by 1990.[3] There are more malnourished in rural areas (approximately 1.1 billion in 1975),[4] but the incidence is accelerating more rapidly in urban areas. Furthermore, the degree of malnutrition among urban dwellers is frequently more severe than among their rural counterparts.

Although urban malnutrition to a certain extent reflects the shift to the cities of the rural malnourished, natural growth in the number of urban poor accounts increasingly for the spread of malnutrition in the cities. While rural development and nutrition intervention in the countryside will continue to be of key importance, the growing problem of urban poverty and malnutrition must be confronted directly and urgently. Accelerated development in the countryside will not eliminate urban malnutrition, but human capital erosion and individual deprivation caused by urban malnutrition can be alleviated by various types of nutrition intervention. Documentation of nutrition programming experience in urban areas is, however, minimal. Though evidence about the effect of alternative nutrition interventions is insufficient to design a definitive program, the urgency of the problem requires immediate programmatic action. Therefore, within the limitations of available data, this paper attempts to provide a framework for systematically mounting an urban nutrition intervention program and a series of tentative guidelines for designing the various components of such a program.

This study presupposes a government already intends to allocate resources to combat urban malnutrition, and inquires into the most effective use of those resources.[5] It focuses on nutrition and

3. The 200-million figure has been cited as the number of "absolute poor" by Robert McNamara in "The Significance of Habitat," *Finance and Development,* vol. 13, no. 1 (March 1976), p. 5; the other figures are based on calculations by Shlomo Reutlinger of the World Bank.

4. Shlomo Reutlinger and Marcelo Selowsky, *Malnutrition and Poverty: Magnitude and Policy Options,* World Bank Staff Occasional Papers, no. 23 (Baltimore: Johns Hopkins University Press, 1976), derived from Table 13, p. 31.

5. For a discussion of the rationale for mounting nutrition programs see Alan Berg, *The Nutrition Factor* (Washington, D.C.: Brookings Institution, 1973), chaps. 2, 3, and 4; Alan Berg, Nevin Scrimshaw, and David Call (eds.), *Nutrition, National Development and Planning* (Cambridge, Mass.: MIT Press, 1973); and Marcelo Selowsky and Lance Taylor, "The Economics of Malnourished Children: An Example of Disinvestment in Human Capital," *Economic Development and Cultural Change,* vol. 22, no. 1 (October 1973), pp. 17–30.

interventions in urban areas, but, to a great extent, the conceptual framework and many of the analytical techniques apply as well to rural areas. Because problems of urban and rural poverty are inextricably entwined through the flow of people, goods, and services, both problems must be addressed simultaneously and in a coordinated manner. The exclusion from this paper of a discussion of urban-rural links and of primary rural interventions, such as food production, constitutes not a denial of their importance but a reflection of the paper's narrower scope. Finally, the discussion is centered primarily on direct nutrition interventions and only secondarily on ancillary programs, such as health or water projects, which might also enhance nutritional well-being. Since nutrition programming should be coordinated and often explicitly integrated with these programs, integration will be discussed, though the primary scope of this study is restricted to direct urban nutrition programs.

Effective intervention design involves coordination between policy formulation and program implementation. Setting goals, selecting target beneficiaries, shaping and choosing intervention alternatives, and allocating resources all require policy guidance and all carry operating implications. It is hoped that the study, by focusing on intervention design, proves useful to both policymakers and project implementers.

The bulk of this study is concentrated in three chapters.

Chapter 2 examines nutritional deficiencies, causality factors, and target population groups. Multiple nutritional deficiencies affect different groups within the urban populace differently. The relative nutritional vulnerability of individual segments of the population is assessed to specify target groups for nutrition intervention. The group selected and the reasons for its malnutrition fundamentally affect the design of interventions.

Chapter 3 specifies the information about urban environment, economic behavior, and nutritional status indicators that the planner needs. The urban environment subsection emphasizes the need to recognize the relevance of the urban setting and the urbanizing process. In particular it emphasizes demographic and socioeconomic indicators and the institutional and physical infrastructure. Under economic behavior, food habits, the food distribution system, and characteristics of food demand are reviewed. The nutritional status subsection sets forth the relative strengths and limitations of direct and indirect indicators and analyzes their use in the planning of nutrition interventions. A consideration of each category of information attempts to identify the data analysts should collect, the means of collection, and ways to analyze and interpret that data. Relying on existing knowledge and experience, which are often inadequate, tentative judgments are made on the appropriate use of data.

Once information on malnutrition has been collected, an appropriate program can be designed. Chapter 4 analyzes the most important considerations for designing nine possible nutrition programs: nutrition education, on-site feeding, take-home feeding, nutrient-dense foods, ration shops, food coupons, fortification, direct nutrient dosage, and food processing and distribution. In addition, the integration of nutrition and nonnutrition programs (primarily in health, family planning, and water and sanitation) is examined.

Furthermore, means by which planners can evaluate options for nutrition programs are addressed in chapter 5 relative to selection criteria, financial analysis, and cost effectiveness. Chapter 6 focuses on program management by considering problems of control, personnel, publicity, finance, and organization. It also identifies barriers to the implementation of a program.

2

•·•··•·•·

The Malnutrition Problem

The starting point in designing any effective nutrition program is diagnosing the nature of the problem. This chapter will describe the general types of nutritional deficiencies, discuss their causality, and examine the task of selecting the target groups for the nutrition programs.

Types of Nutritional Deficiency

In physiological terms, malnutrition is a pathological state deriving from a relative or absolute deficiency or excess of one or more nutrients. Clinical, anthropometric, and physiological tests discriminate three main forms of malnutrition in developing countries:

- Undernutrition: the pathological state resulting from long-term consumption of an inadequate quantity of food.
- Specific deficiency: the pathological state resulting from a relative or absolute lack of a particular nutrient.
- Imbalance: the pathological state resulting from a disproportionate amount of any nutrient with or without a deficiency of any other nutrient.

In most instances, only undernutrition and specific deficiency are important causes of malnutrition among target groups in developing countries.

Although it is generally accepted that most worldwide nutrient deficiencies are protein and calorie related, many people suffer from other nutrient deficits; specific nutrient deficiencies therefore warrant close attention. Some types of malnutrition—for example, scurvy, pellagra, and beriberi—have become less important problems because reasonably precise knowledge is now available about their epidemiology and cure. Vitamin A deficiency, iron and folate-deficiency anemias, and endemic goiter are, however, still widely prevalent, although goiter is relatively rare in urban areas. The following tabulation summarizes different types of malnutrition in developing countries and the nutrients most often involved:[1]

Disease	*Nutrient lacking*
Protein-calorie malnutrition (PCM)	
Kwashiorkor	Protein
Marasmus	Protein and calories
Mild-to-moderate PCM	Protein and calories
Vitamin-deficiency diseases	
Xerophthalmia	Vitamin A
Beriberi	Vitamin B$_1$
Ariboflavinosis	Vitamin B$_2$
Pellagra	Niacin
Scurvy	Vitamin C
Rickets	Vitamin D
Mineral-deficiency diseases	
Anemia	Iron
Goiter	Iodine
Rickets and osteomalacia	Calcium

An examination of country-specific data reveals that urban dwellers are particularly disadvantaged nutritionally. As shown in Table 2-1, the caloric intake of urban populations is frequently, although not always, less than that of their rural counterparts. When the population is stratified by income levels, the calorie deficit among the urban poor is seen to be larger than that of the rural poor. The relatively inferior nutritional position of urban inhabitants seems also to hold for nutrients other than calories, as is shown in Table 2-2.[2] The more nutritionally needy and vulnerable subgroups within the urban and rural populations are infants, children, and pregnant women. In many countries these groups appear to be even worse off in the urban areas. Indicators of nutritional status, such as anthropometric growth measurements and measurements of deficits of nutrient intake, confirm the relatively

1. Y. Hofvander, "Malnutrition and the Individual," in *Nutrition: A Priority in African Development,* ed. Bo Vahlquist (New York: Dag Hammarskjöld Foundation, 1972).

2. The appendix also discusses these micronutrient deficiencies in more detail.

Table 2-1. *Differences in Average Urban and Rural Caloric Intake,*
Selected Countries

Region	Urban	Rural
West Pakistan	1,806	2,126
East Pakistan	1,732	2,251
Eastern Brazil	2,331	2,258
Southern Brazil	2,451	3,072
India	1,480	2,090
Thailand	1,504	1,821
Trinidad and Tobago	2,550	3,011
Chad	2,113	2,467
Korea, Republic of	1,946	2,181
Indonesia	1,633	1,885

Sources: West Pakistan, S. M. Naseem, "Mass Poverty in Pakistan: Some Preliminary Find-ings," *Pakistan Development Review*, vol. 8, no. 4 (Winter 1973), pp. 317–60. East Pakistan, U.S. Department of Health, Education, and Welfare, *Pakistan: Nutrition Survey of E. Pakistan, 1962–64* (Washington, D.C.: Public Health Service, May 1966). Eastern Brazil, The Getúlio Vargas Foundation, *Food Consumption in Brazil: Family Budget Surveys in Early 1960s* (Rio de Janeiro, November 1970). Southern Brazil and India, D. N. Basu, "Consumption Patterns and Life Styles: 2000 A.D." (Baroda: Operations Research Group, January 1975), pp. 39–40 (kilocalories from food grains only). Thailand, V. Pisolyabutra, "Basic Data for Assessment of Nutritional Status of Thailand" (Bangkok: Nutrition Planning Group, National Social and Economic Devel-opment Board, August 1974). Trinidad and Tobago, Caribbean Food and Nutrition Institute, "Report on the National Household Food Consumption Survey in Trinidad and Tobago," Octo-ber 1970, as reported by Samir S. Basta, "Nutrition and Health in Low-Income Urban Areas of the Third World," *Ecology of Food and Nutrition*, vol. 6 (1977), p. 118. Chad, Minister du Plan et de la Coopération, *Enquête Socio-économique du Chad, 1965* (Paris, September 1969), as reported by Basta in *Ecology of Food and Nutrition*, p. 118. Republic of Korea, "A Report of Nutrition Survey, 1969," *Korean Journal of Nutrition*, vol. 3, no. 1 (1970), as reported by Basta in *Ecology of Food and Nutrition*, p. 118. Indonesia, W. van Ginneken, *Rural and Urban Income In-equalities in Indonesia, Mexico, Pakistan, Tanzania, and Tunisia* (Geneva: International Labour Of-fice, 1976).

disadvantageous nutritional position of the urban poor. For ex-ample, anthropometric results show that middle-class and rural Thai boys have mean heights and weights fully equal to the North American standard of the 50th percentile during the first six months of life, but that urban slum Thai boys are well below the 50th percentile in weight during the first six months and fall below the third percentile during the second six months of life.[3] Even more alarming than these height and weight discrepancies is the fact that the proportion of children from the slums of Bangkok with PCM in the 0- to 5-month and 6- to 11-month age group are enormously high compared with the rural population. It is not

3. Pensri Khanjansthiti and Joe Wray. "Early Protein-Calorie Malnutrition in the Slum Areas of Bangkok Municipality 1970–1971," (Bangkok: Ramathibodi Hospi-tal, 1972), p. 6.

Table 2-2. *Per Capita Nutrient Intake in Urban and Rural Areas, West Pakistan*

Nutrient	Urban	Rural	Recommended
Calories	1,806	2,126	2,067–2,088
Protein (grams)	58.4	69.8	58.5–59.5
Fat (grams)	41.3	40.8	—
Carbohydrate (grams)	300.2	369.9	—
Calcium (milligrams)	356.6	369.9	465
Iron (milligrams)	16.1	20.5	106.6–11.9
Vitamin A (international units)	1,610.0	1,731.0	2,985–3,042
Thiamin (milligrams)	1.59	2.05	0.83
Riboflavin (milligrams)	0.64	0.79	0.83
Niacin (milligrams)	17.9	21.7	13.7
Vitamin C (milligrams)	22.5	28.0	28.2

Source: S. M. Naseem, "Mass Poverty in Pakistan: Some Preliminary Findings," *Pakistan Development Review,* vol. 8, no. 4 (Winter 1973), pp. 317–60.

until the second year of life that the mean heights and weights of rural and slum children become similar, as the familiar flattening of the growth curve is seen in the postweaning period.

Causality

Urban malnutrition is fundamentally a manifestation of a larger syndrome, urban poverty. Nonetheless, since other factors impinge on malnutrition, its multiple etiology should be investigated in order to assess the extent to which an intervention is attacking a cause or a symptom. The most common causes fall into four principal categories.

Low incomes

When total family diets reveal consumption levels substantially below minimum requirements, low income is the basic cause, especially in conjunction with high unemployment, underemployment, or low wages. Urban unemployment rates are high. One survey found that one-third of the countries had rates over 15 percent and two-thirds over 8 percent; the rates in the 15–24 age group were 10 percent to 40 percent.[4]

4. Paul Bairoch, *Urban Unemployment in Developing Countries* (Geneva: International Labour Office, 1973), pp. 51–52. Measures to increase employment are central to alleviating urban deprivation but will not be dealt with in this paper.

Food-system deficiencies

The food system affects purchasing power through prices and diets through the products it offers. The urban poor are particularly vulnerable to market forces because, unlike their rural counterparts, they are almost totally dependent on the commercial marketplace for their food. Consequently, costly inefficiencies in the food system, including storage and handling losses or nutritionally adverse promotional or processing practices, are areas of concern.

Sociocultural beliefs

Even if the income constraint could be mitigated, nutritional deficiencies arising from mistaken beliefs and practices about food and health still remain. Where family dietary intake levels approach recommended minimum allowances, groups within the families (particularly youngest children) may still suffer nutritional deficits. Analysts should be aware of potentially harmful weaning practices or feeding beliefs during child illness (such as food withdrawal), or during pregnancy (such as protein abstention), or intrafamilial food distribution practices (such as preference to adult males). In addition, urban socialization may involve sociological pressure to adopt nutritionally harmful practices (such as acquiring high-cost status foods or decreasing breastfeeding). Working mothers may have to leave their young children in the care of older children, who are less able to attend to the nutritional needs of the younger siblings.

Unfavorable health environment

The urban poor more than likely lack adequate water, sewerage, and health care. Congestion and crowding further exacerbate the health environment and increase the probability of infectious diseases. Although such sicknesses and nutritional shortfalls may not be too severe alone, together their effect can be fatal, especially for young children.

The nutrition planner should attempt to diagnose malnutrition's multiple causality fully and, to the extent possible, address these causes jointly through a multifaceted plan for intervention.

Selection of the Target Group

Although all segments of the population evidently can suffer nutritional deficiencies, specific segments are more vulnerable and, in fact, more severely affected. It is generally recognized that the group most at nutritional risk comprises preschool-age children.[5] Those under 3 years of age are particularly exposed because of heightened nutrient requirements during this period of accelerated growth. Pregnant and lactating women are also nutritionally at risk because of their increased nutrient needs during pregnancy and lactation, and because of the deleterious effect their malnutrition can have on birth weights and the survival and nutritional well-being of newborns and infants. In 1975 an estimated 59 million children under 5 and 22 million pregnant and lactating women in urban areas were incurring calorie deficits. By the year 2000 the numbers will rise, respectively, to 122 million and 40 million.

Nutritional deprivation in the earliest years of life constitutes the greatest threat of mortality and impairment of physical and mental development. Children under 5 account for the majority of total deaths in most developing countries, and malnutrition is a primary or associated cause of most of these fatalities.[6] Older children and adults are physiologically more able to cope with nutritional deficits, which are less threatening to life and health, but such deficiencies can adversely affect performance in school or at work. Certain deficiencies, such as iron and folate anemias, can particularly diminish worker productivity and they therefore merit priority attention.

The concept of nutritional vulnerability offers one way of establishing priorities for nutrition interventions. Because of competing demands for their limited funds, governments cannot generally satisfy every nutritional need of the population. The nutrition planner must therefore allocate available funds among groups within the population. The criterion of nutritional need ordinarily gives top priority to children under 3 and to pregnant and lactating women because of their greater nutritional need and the far-reaching consequences of their malnutrition. Nonetheless, other groups such as the iron-deficient workers mentioned above might also be identified as needy.

5. Derrick B. Jelliffe, *The Assessment of the Nutritional Status of the Community* (Geneva: World Health Organization [WHO], 1966), p. 176; and *Child Health in the Tropics*, 3rd ed. (London: Edward Arnold Ltd., 1969), p. 7.

6. For example, in Latin America malnutrition was a primary cause of 8 percent and an associated cause of 46 percent of the deaths of children under 5; the related causes were measles, diarrhea, other infective or parasitic diseases, and respiratory ailments. Pan American Health Organization, *Inter-American Investigation of Mortality in Childhood*, cited in Alan Berg, *The Nutrition Factor* (Washington, D.C.: Brookings Institution, 1973), p. 225.

Recuperation of nutritionally deficient groups is a basic goal, but care should be taken to keep the main thrust of the interventions preventive rather than curative. Prevention consists in keeping currently malnourished individuals from further deterioration and preventing healthy but risk-prone individuals such as preschoolers from low-income families from becoming malnourished. Dietary supplementation for pregnant women is essentially a preventive intervention.

The economic—as contrasted to the obviously humanitarian—rationale for using nutritional vulnerability criteria rests on the notion of investment in human capital. Prevention of death or physical and mental retardation improves the quantity and quality of a nation's human stock and therefore increases productive potential. Other criteria would orient programs toward other groups. For example, feeding schoolchildren might be supported as a means of realizing a return on the nation's educational investment by improving classroom performance. Similarly, if nutritional deficiencies limit output, nutritional supplementation for working adults might be justified according to the productivity criterion. Finally, as in all decisions on the allocation of resources, political criteria will influence the selection of target groups.

The targeting of interventions has significant implications economically and for program design.[7] Targeting attempts to channel limited funds to groups who will benefit most. Rather than dilute the efficacy of available funds by trying to cover large groups, the intervention planner services fewer but needier people by concentrating resources. This targeting process can be illustrated by the following example.

In a hypothetical city population of 500,000, the planners estimate from demographic data the number of children under 3 years of age (13 percent of population, or 65,000) and pregnant and lactating women (4 percent of population, or 20,000). A point of reference now exists against which to match available resources. If US$500,000 has been allocated, only $1.00 per capita is available if the program is to serve the entire population of 500,000.[8] But if children under 3 and pregnant and lactating women were to make up the target groups, the planners would have $5.88 per capita to

7. Shlomo Reutlinger and Marcelo Selowsky, *Malnutrition and Poverty: Magnitude and Policy Options*, World Bank Staff Occasional Papers, no. 23 (Baltimore: Johns Hopkins University Press, 1976), pp. 49–52.

8. In this study all amounts are quoted in U.S. dollars.

dispense. Calculations might reveal that worthwhile nutritional improvement would cost $10.00 per capita. At this unit cost, the potential target group could not be adequately covered. Consequently, either total resources would have to be increased or the target group narrowed. To narrow, the planner might restrict the intervention to children who manifest growth deficiencies according to anthropometric standards: that is, second- or third-degree malnutrition. This criterion might reduce by half the group under 3 to receive assistance. Furthermore, 20 percent of the pregnant and lactating women could probably dispense with participation in the program because of their higher income and educational levels. The target group would then number 48,500, permitting a resource allocation of $10.30 per capita based on the original budget appropriation. This amount would improve the prospects of achieving success in the nutrition program.

Targeting inevitably leads to a discussion of program design. Designation of a target group influences the type of intervention to be selected, the form of nutritional supplement to be used, and the location and timing of the intervention. Examples will clarify these assertions. If a vitamin A deficiency is prevalent across age groups in much of the population, it might be appropriate to fortify a widely consumed staple, as is done with sugar in Guatemala and Costa Rica. This choice would be less appropriate if the deficiency afflicts restricted age and geographic groups rather than the general population. If the deficiency is PCM and the target group is children under 3, a special weaning food might be employed as a dietary supplement. Health clinics, hospitals, and midwives can assist pregnant and lactating women before and after delivery. Income criteria might suggest concentration of delivery systems in slum neighborhoods.

To summarize, targeting makes more cost-effective use of limited resources. Nutritional vulnerability should be the dominant criterion in establishing priorities among target groups. Although other groups can be differently affected by various nutritional deficiencies, young children and pregnant and lactating women from low-income families generally constitute the most nutritionally vulnerable groups. In selecting target groups, the planners should delineate the design and cost implications of their choice. Circumstances may force a change in the designation of a program's beneficiaries, but such modification of the goals of a program must be based on more complete information, which is considered in the next chapter.

3

•━•••━•

Informational
Requirements

Many approaches to nutrition planning have been postulated in recent years.[1] Although they vary in emphasis and methodology, all have common elements. They generally start with problem diagnosis, which leads to the designation of alternatives for intervention. The alternatives are in turn evaluated so a final nutrition program can be selected and implemented.

Data needs vary in each of the five stages of the nutrition-planning process: problem diagnosis, strategy formulation, intervention design, program implementation, and performance evaluation. Problem diagnosis is the door to the process. The basic objective is to get as little information as is necessary to make reasonable judgments. The following elementary diagnostic questions should be answered by the analyst from information gathered on the urban environment and on the economic behavior and nutritional status of its inhabitants.

What is the type and severity of nutritional deficiencies affecting the target group? The nutritional deficiencies of principal concern in ur-

Note: My coauthors for the following sections of this chapter in the original report to the World Bank were: "Informational Category 1: The Urban Environment," Judith McGuire, Johanna Dwyer, Bea Rogers, and Marian Zeitlin; "Food habits," Judith McGuire and Johanna Dwyer; "Food demand," Dave Wheeler, John Harris, and Gordon Rausser; "Informational Category 3: Nutritional Status," Marian Zeitlin, Barbara Millen Posner, Eileen Kennedy, D. Mark Hegsted, Stanley Gershoff, and M. Guillermo Herrera.

1. Alan Berg, *The Nutrition Factor* (Washington, D.C.: Brookings Institution, 1973), Appendix D, pp. 233–47; J. Leonard Joy and P. R. Payne, *Food and Nutrition Planning*, Food and Agricultural Organizations (FAO) Nutrition Consultants Report Series no. 35 (Rome: FAO, 1975); Joint FAO/WHO Expert Committee on Nutrition, *Food and Nutrition Strategies in National Development*, FAO Nutrition Meetings, Report Series no. 56 (Rome: FAO, 1976).

ban centers are likely to be protein-calorie malnutrition (PCM), but micronutrient deficiencies (for example, of vitamins A and B and of iron) are also important. Careful surveys are needed to diagnose conditions resulting from nutritional deficiencies. The economic behavior section, below, will present a method of determining deficit levels by relating income levels to deficits. Surveys of the intake of food during a twenty-four-hour period are helpful in calculating the deficits, but they generally do not involve income data. As the nutritional status section makes clear, intake and deficit estimates are only indirect approximations. More direct indicators of nutritional severity are anthropometric data and vital statistics, which may already exist or can be gathered by sample survey in the nutritionally vulnerable zones of the city. This basic information should be assembled at the start of any project.

Data gathered on household expenditure, as well as information on food habits, will answer a second general diagnostic question: *what are the basic causes of malnutrition?* Understanding the causes is a prerequisite to designing an effective intervention. As previously suggested, the primary constraint on a healthy diet is likely to be lack of income, but ignorance of the nutritional value of food, social attitudes and practices, poor health, and lack of sanitation may also be significant factors. If food intervention is to be the remedy, understanding the dynamics of the food system and of household behavior is essential.

The next question is: *who is affected?* The analyst can start with the presumption that the nutritionally vulnerable will be the poorest families and the most at-risk family members will be the children under 3 and the pregnant and lactating women. Nutrition programming requires, however, specificity and quantification to determine resource requirements. This need leads to a third question: *how many malnourished are there?* To answer this query, the analyst can look initially at the demography, infrastructure, and census statistics considered in the urban environment section. These data should answer a fourth question: *where are the malnourished?* Knowledge of where they live will also help in estimating the size of population in low-income areas. Data on family composition from census statistics or family planning studies permit calculation of the numbers of preschoolers and pregnant and lactating women.

Interventions can be undertaken on the basis of the deficits revealed by food expenditure or intake surveys or by growth retardation data and high infant and preschooler mortality rates. Both forms of data should be gathered, since both are needed to pin-point target families and to assess the severity of their deficiencies. Unless it is known how many people are suffering and to what extent, it is impossible to answer the fundamental question about intervention design: *what is the quantity and type of incremental nutrients or the behavioral or institutional change that the nutrition intervention needs to provide?* This estimate is basic to determining the cost of the urban nutrition program.

The three categories of information to be considered in this section are (a) characteristics of the urban environment, (b) economic behavior, and (c) nutritional status.

The widest category of required information concerns the nature of the urban environment: that is, the demographic, sociological, physical, and institutional characteristics prevailing in urban areas. Certain easily identifiable aspects of the urban environment may be useful correlates of malnutrition. Before the program is designed, data on urban environmental characteristics can offer planners an approximate and inexpensive means for an initial assessment of the malnutrition problem and identification of the most vulnerable groups. Later the planners will use this information to design systems to reach the malnourished groups.

To comprehend the roots of malnutrition among low-income groups and to identify the means of eradicating it, an examination is necessary of the positive and negative effects on nutritional status of the total food economy, including food supply and demand, prices, processing and handling, and dietary habits and preferences. Indicators of nutritional status are essential to the diagnosis of the problem and the evaluation of the program. Precise determination of the nutritional status of the entire population is not economically feasible nor is it necessary, yet a reasonably accurate diagnosis of the status of preschool children and pregnant and lactating women is basic to intervention design.

A detailed consideration of each of these categories of information will be given below, and the relative desirability of alternative types of data, data collection, and analysis procedures will be judged. The value of originating surveys to collect new data should be evaluated against the criteria: the cost of collecting and analyzing the data; the time needed to gather and analyze it; the skills and facilities required to gather and process the information; and the reliability, accuracy, and validity of the data generated.

Informational Category 1: The Urban Environment

Certain demographic, socioeconomic, and infrastructural characteristics of the city can be put to two uses: the identification of the
target group and the design of the intervention. In the early planning stages it is wise to estimate quickly the location of the nutritionally vulnerable urban groups, their numbers, and the severity
of their nutritional risk. Approximate estimates from existing data
provide a first rough assessment of the problem and define the
need for further information. Several urban characteristics appear
to be predictive of nutritional risk because they would seem to be
correlates of both malnutrition and poverty. In the existing litera-
ture of research on urbanization and nutritional status, no quan-
titative examination considers the precise links between urban
characteristics and malnutrition. Because the degree of selectivity
and predictability of these indicators is not known, the relation between the city and malnutrition remains an important item for further research. The subsequent consideration of correlates of urban
malnutrition must therefore be viewed as a set of hypotheses in
need of empirical verification.

A listing and examination of potential risk indicators can perhaps facilitate for other researchers the task of verification. These
risk indicators also provide a useful checklist for planners as they
make their first assessment of the problem. Planners can make
more precise estimates of the problem from the economic-behavior
variables and the more direct nutritional status indicators. Despite
the lack of precision of urban characteristics as correlates of malnutrition, this information is valuable in selecting the type of intervention and its design. Effective design of intervention requires
recognition and treatment of environmental factors that either
help or hinder the implementation of a nutrition program.

A preliminary judgment, based on predictive value and information availability, suggests that the best indicators are population
density and growth measures, migration as a percentage of total
population growth, birth order, dependency ratio, water and sewerage connection rates, and health facilities per habitant.

It is doubtful that one indicator can adequately locate and quantify target groups. Combining different indicators appears to increase their predictive value, although only experimentation will
disclose the best combination.

The following description of predictors of malnutrition and other environmental characteristics considers their use in identifying target groups and designing the intervention. The selected environmental characteristics fall into two principal categories: (a) demographic and socioeconomic, and (b) physical and institutional.

Demographic and socioeconomic characteristics

Useful demographic and socioeconomic indicators concern population density and growth, migration, family size, family structure, maternal employment, and parental literacy.

DENSITY AND GROWTH OF POPULATION. Statistics on population density are helpful in locating the general target population because the most vulnerable population is often found where population density is highest. For example, population density in slum areas in Calcutta and Manila is four or five times higher than the averages for the entire city.[2] Density statistics also carry implications for intervention design, since higher density allows precise geographic targeting. Concentration simplifies the logistics of delivery, allows closer control, and yields economies from the more intense use of facilities, equipment, and personnel.

Another helpful indicator is household density, defined by either square meters of floor space or the number of rooms per household member. For example, Bangkok slums average about 3.5 people per room, far above the city norm.[3] Household-density statistics are less frequently available than general density statistics, but if available they pinpoint families at risk. Higher household density results in crowding and increased pressure on sanitary facilities, with accompanying adverse effects on disease generation and transmittal. High density also probably indicates lower income, which is also associated with greater nutritional vulnerability.

In addition to examining density figures, the analyst should look at population growth rates. Cities and zones within cities experi-

2. "Socioeconomic Survey Report" (Manila, 1974); World Bank, *India Calcutta Urban Development Project, Background Studies of Calcutta Metropolitan District*, Report no. 205-N (Washington, D.C., 1973), pp. 1–41.

3. Susan Morell and David Morell, *Six Slums in Bangkok: Problems of Life and Options for Action* (Bangkok: United Nations Children's Fund [UNICEF], 1972), Table I-10, p. 12.

encing disproportionately accelerating population growth, whether the consequence of natural increase or immigration, are probably also witnessing a decline in the health environment because of increased pressures on health services and housing. High growth rates, especially if coincident with high density rates, are good locators of target neighborhoods. For example, although Manila City grew at a rate of 1.5 percent a year between 1960 and 1970, the slum areas of Mandaluyong, Caloocan City, and Quezon City expanded at a rate of 7 percent.[4] In addition, the analyst needs growth rates to project the future size of the at-risk population and to estimate more accurately resource requirements. Combining density and growth rates increases their predictive utility.[5]

MIGRATION. Migrants, especially recent arrivals from rural areas, appear to be a particularly vulnerable group because they are frequently at a social, psychological, economic, and physical disadvantage. The planner should therefore examine their characteristics and behavioral patterns with care.

The first relevant statistic is the magnitude of the migration. A large influx of migrants immediately designates vulnerable cities and neighborhoods.[6] A more relevant but less available statistic is the proportion of migrants within the disadvantaged population. Because migration statistics are often unavailable from census data,

---

4. World Bank, *Urban Sector Survey, Manila* (Washington, D.C., 1975), Table III, p. 12.

5. Beware the pitfalls that come from looking at a single indicator. For example, Cali, Colombia, and Calcutta slums show below average growth rates, suggesting lower risk. An examination of the population density statistics, however, reveals rates four to six times greater than city averages—a clear indication of vulnerability. Rather than low nutritional risk, the low growth rates probably indicate a more mature or stabilized poverty zone jammed to physical capacity. They may also, incidentally, suggest that new poverty areas are expanding in other zones within or just outside the city.

6. In São Paulo it was estimated that, of the 3.2 percent a year population growth between 1920 and 1940, 1.6 percent could be attributed to migration. In the following decades, the growth was 6.3 percent a year, of which 4.0 percent was caused by migration; Escola Paulista de Medicina, Instituto de Medicina Preventiva, Universidade de São Paulo, Instituto de Pesquisas Econômicas, *Estado Nutricional de Crianças de 6 à Mêses no Município de São Paulo*, vol. 2, *Análise de Datos* (São Paulo: Ministério de Educação e Cultura, 1975), p. 2. Hereafter cited as Escola Paulista, *Estado Nutricional*.

sample surveys may be necessary.[7] The leaders of a migrant community should be asked the size, characteristics, and location of their community, and should be consulted on the nature of the community's problems and possible solutions to them. Participation at the community level in the planning process is in itself a valuable development goal; it is also an important means of ensuring congruity with community needs and of eliciting local support essential to the program's success. Squatter or migrant organizations are common in Latin America; often they are politically powerful, as are the Derneks in Turkey.[8] Frequently, these groups have strong ethnic links to certain regions or towns, as do the tribal unions found in some African cities. Consequently, they may also act as a conduit to the rural areas for the dissemination of nutrition education or of information on nutrition services.

Information on migration should be examined with an eye to the ethnic composition of a city. Different ethnic groups may have different migratory and employment patterns. Ethnic origin may create a position amounting to caste status within a city, since citizens favor "their own people" where social services and employment opportunities are scarce. Certain ethnic groups—and caste groups within ethnic groups—may be particularly vulnerable nutritionally because they are discriminated against across the board, they live in inferior housing in poorly serviced sections of the town, and they suffer from unusually high unemployment. Furthermore, language, food preferences, food and health beliefs, and lifestyle decisions affecting the marginal propensity for food consumption all vary by ethnic origin. These differences should be scrutinized in designing programs in nutrition education and in choosing food for feeding programs or subsidization.[9]

Another useful statistic on migrants is the time elapsed since their arrival. This information constitutes a crude indicator of income, employment, and access to services, because migrants, espe-

7. Sidney Goldstein and David Sly, *Basic Data Needed for the Study of Urbanization*, (Liège, Belgium: Ordina Editions, International Union for the Scientific Study of Population, 1974), p. 12.

8. Joan M. Nelson, "Sojourners versus New Urbanites: Causes and Consequences of Temporary versus Permanent Cityward Migration in Developing Countries," *Economic Development and Cultural Change* (July 1976), pp. 750–57.

9. For example, such heterogeneity is well illustrated in many cities in India; see Hindustan Thompson Associates, *A Study of Food Habits in Calcutta* (Calcutta: Lalchand Roy and Co. Ltd., 1969), p. 10.

cially recent migrants, tend to work in low-paying, unskilled occu-
pations in the informal sector and are often unaware of the services
available to them. It is important to incorporate new arrivals into
any scheme devoted to nutritional improvement because of their
potential high risk and possible reticence to seek help. Traditional
means of serving urban dwellers (through dispensaries and existing social services) may not reach these persons.

A subset of recent arrivals are temporary migrants who come to
the city for a brief period with the expectation of returning to the
country. They frequently come to earn extra income for special
purchases, such as farm equipment, housing improvements, and
brides. These migrants are often single males, particularly in Africa and South and East Asia. For example, the male-to-female ratios of migrants in several cities are: Kinshasa, 1.72; Istanbul, 1.43;
Karachi, 1.47; Delhi, 1.42; Bombay, 1.97; and Calcutta, 2.92.[10] The
sex ratio may serve as a measure of temporary migration. Where
this ratio is high the nutritional vulnerability of the migrant group
would be less because the more nutritionally vulnerable family
members, the preschoolers and mothers, would still be in the countryside (and perhaps particularly vulnerable there). The transient
nature of temporary migrants also means that they tend to place
fewer demands on services such as health care. Moreover, some of
these individuals might become disseminators of nutritional education upon their return to the country. This pattern does not hold,
however, for most Latin American cities; in fact, the ratios are reversed, with women dominating—for example, 0.79 in Bogotá,
0.82 in Mexico City, and 0.89 in Caracas.[11] These figures may reflect the migration of young women seeking work as domestics.
Clearly, this group of potential mothers is of concern because of
the inherent nutritional risks of pregnancy and motherhood.

For more established slum families, permanent delivery systems,
such as health clinics and ration shops, in the low-income areas are
a more effective approach. It is both incorrect and counterproductive to perceive slums as unstable, transitory phenomena
that do not warrant permanent intervention. For many, the slum is
a permanent neighborhood. For example, a survey of one Bangkok slum shows that 61 percent of the residents had lived there
longer than seven years and only 12 percent had lived there less

10. Nelson, "Sojourners versus New Urbanites," p. 727.
11. Ibid.

than one year.[12] The transience of urban dwellers may not be as large a problem for intervention design as is generally believed. Squatter settlements frequently manifest considerable capacity for self-improvement as, for example, in the continued upgrading of their housing. These economically marginal populations have considerable productive potential frequently overlooked by planners. There is growing evidence that direct assistance intended to improve existing squatter settlements through the provision of basic services (which could include nutrition) can significantly improve the quality of life. Such improvements appear to be within the realm of financial feasibility. Slum and squatter upgrading projects are being carried out successfully, for example, in Indonesia and in Zambia at a per capita cost of about $40 and $35 respectively.[13]

FAMILY SIZE AND STRUCTURE. Household size is an inconsistent indicator of poverty because larger families frequently have higher incomes. A study of ten Latin American cities found that average household size of families in the highest income quartile always exceeded that in the lowest (6.35 as against 5.20), but households of nine or more members are more frequent in the lowest and third quartile and are rare in the upper-income quartile.[14] Where large household size and low income coincide, nutritional and health status are usually low. In a São Paulo survey the malnourished children were more frequently found in the larger families in the low-income bracket.[15] Data on household size are primarily needed for program estimates only after the target group has been identified. A better correlate of malnutrition is family size.

The term "family size" refers to the number of children in the family, including those of relatives who may be part of an extended family sharing one home. The relation between nutrition and number of children is clearer than the relation between nutrition

12. Morell and Morell, *Six Slums*, Table III-3. For an especially insightful view of the realities of the sociology of slums, see Janice E. Perlman, *The Myth of Marginality: Urban Poverty and Politics in Rio de Janeiro* (Berkeley: University of California Press, 1976).

13. Callisto Eneas Madavo, "Uncontrolled Settlements," *Finance and Development*, vol. 13, no. 1 (March 1976), p. 19.

14. Philip Musgrove, *Consumer Behavior in Latin America: Income and Spending of Families in Ten Andean Cities* (Washington, D.C.: Brookings Institution, 1978), pp. 65–71.

15. Escola Paulista, *Estado Nutricional*, p. 42.

and household size. Throughout the world, except in the middle and upper classes, the nutritional status of children (measured by growth) tends to decline with birth order.[16]

Children of higher birth order (that is, born later) tend to be less well nourished because the mother's nutritional resources have been depleted by successive pregnancies and lactation periods, parents have less time to give to the care of the infant, and the limited food supply will have to be stretched to feed more family members. Thus, the birth order of four or more children is a useful indicator of nutritional risk. A related indicator is the short birth interval between siblings, which also increases nutritional risk because the mother's physical resources cannot recover completely between closely spaced pregnancies, and her attention is almost immediately divided between two or more children.

The age variable in the family structure should also be considered. The population in all developing countries is weighted heavily toward the young: more than half are under 15 years of age. It appears that lower-income groups are characterized by higher youth populations that increase the dependency load and therefore the economic burden. A study of the low-income areas of Tondo and Foreshore in Manila, for example, disclosed that 64 percent of the population was under 20 years of age, whereas in the Manila metropolitan area only 47 percent were in that age group.[17] In the Bangkok slums the group under 14 made up 45 percent of the slum population.[18]

The relatively high youth population among poor families exacerbates the dependency ratio, the number of economically inactive household members (those aged less than 15 and older than 64) divided by total members (the number between 15 and 64). This ratio indicates higher food need and lower effective demand. Families with high dependency ratios need to be identified, since they are at higher risk of malnutrition. In Manila the dependency

16. Niel Christiansen, José O. Mora, and M. Guillermo Herrera, "Family Social Characteristics Related to Physical Growth of Young Children," *British Journal of Preventive Social Medicine*, vol. 29 (1975), pp. 121–30.

17. Samir S. Basta, "Nutrition and Health in Low-Income Urban Areas of the Third World," *Ecology of Food and Nutrition*, vol. 6 (1977), pp. 113–24. The article contains information given in "Draft Report to Manila Urban Development Project," Report no. 1032a-PH (Washington, D.C.: World Bank, 1976), a restricted-circulation document.

18. Morell and Morell, *Six Slums*, Tables II-2 and III-3.

ratio was 67 percent, whereas it was 78 percent in the Tondo areas and 82 percent in the Foreshore.[19] Dependency ratios might be more predictive of family nutritional risk than family size, but large family size coupled with a high dependency ratio constitutes an even stronger verification of nutritional vulnerability. The high unemployment rates among those 15–24 years old further exacerbates the burden of dependency.

A final fact about family structure particularly relevant to intervention design is that its stability affects income, quality of parental care, and social status, all of which impinge on nutritional status. Therefore, it is helpful to be familiar with the mix of family patterns and conjugal unions which underlie family stability. Slum families in developing countries are not necessarily characterized by the stereotypes of single-parent families, disorganization, child neglect, and instability. In the Bangkok slums only 13 percent were single-parent families.[20] In low-income areas of Cali, Colombia, 89 percent of household heads were joined by legal or common law marriages.[21] Still, households headed by females are generally at high risk.[22]

MATERNAL EMPLOYMENT. Working mothers are common in low-income urban areas. For example, although in other areas the percentage is much lower, more than half the mothers in low-income families studied in Bangkok slums work,[23] and the proportion is similar in Rio de Janeiro.[24] The nutritional consequences of the employment of mothers are ambivalent. On the negative side, employment may decrease breastfeeding and leave young children in the hands of inadequate caretakers such as older siblings. On the positive side, the additional income might improve the family diet sufficiently to improve nutritional well-being. Although the ab-

19. "Socioeconomic Survey Report," p. 24.

20. Morell and Morell, *Six Slums*, Tables III-4 and III-2.

21. Beatrice J. Selwyn, "Use and Nonuse of Child Health Services in Cali, Colombia," (Ph.D. dissertation, Tulane University, New Orleans, 1974).

22. Marian Zeitlin and others, "Breastfeeding and Nutritional Status in Depressed Urban Areas of Greater Manila, Philippines," *Ecology of Food and Nutrition* (September 1978), pp. 103–13.

23. Morell and Morell, *Six Slums,* Table III-12.

24. The Getúlio Vargas Foundation, Brazilian Institute of Economics, Division of Econometric Statistics, *Pesquisa sôbre Consumo Alimentar* (Rio de Janeiro, 1975), p. 71.

sence of empirical evidence leaves unknown the net nutritional significance of maternal employment, knowledge of the percentage of working mothers in the target groups is relevant for intervention design. Educational messages about nutrition should be directed at the primary caretaker, who may not be the mother. If many mothers work, day-care facilities can serve as a setting for a nutritional program.

PARENTAL LITERACY. The literacy rate of parents has value as a predictor of risk and is highly relevant in designing programs for nutrition education. For example, in the lowest-income groups in São Paulo the father's illiteracy was much higher in families with malnourished children.[25] This rate is imperfectly related to the educational level, which in turn is correlated with employment and income levels. Maternal literacy rate is an essential ingredient in the selection of the appropriate medium for programs in nutrition education.

Physical and institutional environment

The foregoing demographic and socioeconomic indicators relate primarily to people and their behavior. Since nutritional risk and intervention design are also determined by physical and institutional environment, services such as water, sewerage, electricity, housing, transport, schools, and health are of particular interest to the planner.

WATER. The presence of foul, stagnant water used for garbage and human waste disposal increases children's chances of contracting waterborne diseases. Because slums and squatter settlements are generally situated on the periphery of cities, they are frequently beyond the reach of public water services. For example, only 28 percent of the inhabitants of the Tondo-Foreshore[26] and 38 percent of the low-income group in São Paulo[27] had access to piped water. In addition, slum communities customarily spring up on marginal lands such as floodplains and wetlands and along the sides of ravines, where the extension of public services is difficult.

25. Escola Paulista, *Estado Nutricional,* pp. 43–44.
26. "Socioeconomic Survey Report," pp. 5, 11.
27. Escola Paulista, *Estado Nutricional,* p. 29.

If this difficulty is surmounted and water mains are accessible, the cost of connecting the individual dwelling to the main remains a problem. Even if the cost of water from the municipal mains is far below the price demanded by street vendors, slum dwellers frequently lack the lump sum required to connect their households. In Cali, Colombia, the price of water purchased from a vendor was about 9.6 times greater than the price of an equal volume of tap water.[28] In the Klong Toey slum in Bangkok the median cost per month of water was equivalent to four days' wages.[29] At these prices, water becomes a significant item in the family's food budget, diverting scarce income from other food purchases.

Water-service data from the local water company can identify vulnerable groups quite accurately. Although illegal connections can be common enough to make company statistics underestimates, neighborhoods with low water-connection rates are high-risk areas. An even more discriminating indicator on the family level is access to potable drinking water. Where rates are low, it can also be assumed that the economic burden of acquiring water through other means is onerous.

SEWERAGE. Inadequately disposed sewerage transmits disease by contaminating surface and groundwater and by causing the eutrophication of standing water. Diarrhea, typhoid, cholera, hepatitis, and polio may be acquired by drinking contaminated water. Drainage and runoff from storms, periodic floods, and erosion commonly exacerbate the sewerage-disposal problem in the slums. In the poorest section of Calcutta there was no sewerage at all, whereas 54 percent of the Calcutta Corporation has adequate sewers.[30] In Manila there are 29 sewer connections for each 1,000 people, although in the Tondo District the connection rate is only 15 per 1,000.[31] In São Paulo, 57 percent of the households studied were connected to sewers, whereas 41 percent used ditches.[32]

Accordingly, the sewerage-connection rate is a universally available and useful identifier of target neighborhoods, although it is possibly less precise than the water-connection rate. In combina-

28. Selwyn, "Use and Nonuse," p. 197.
29. Morell and Morell, Six Slums, pp. 15–20.
30. World Bank, India Calcutta Urban Development Project, pp. I-20, I-53.
31. World Bank (1975), Urban Sector Survey, Table III-18, p. III-9 ff.
32. Escola Paulista, Estado Nutricional, pp. 30–31.

tion, these two indicators are reasonably discriminating. Low rates imply low income and a particularly unfavorable sanitary and health environment. Where cities have only minimal public sewerage, information on latrine availability is also relevant.

ELECTRICITY. The availability of electricity does not appear to be a good indicator of nutritional status. Because radio and television are useful media for disseminating education programs, however, some information about electricity and the penetration of the mass media is needed. It is estimated, for example, that from one-quarter to one-third of the slum residences in Bangkok have television, and a higher percentage have radio.[33] In the Tondo-Foreshore of Manila, 82 percent of the household heads listen to radio, compared with 93 percent in all the Philippines and 85 percent in greater Manila. This suggests that mass media might be an efficient vehicle for education about urban nutrition.

HOUSING. A study of the quality of housing and the nature of housing arrangements is useful in target-neighborhood identification. Poor housing, after all, is the most visible sign of a low-income area. Housing studies define quality by such factors as the presence or absence of floors and permanent walls and the type of roofing. These criteria can be used to differentiate among low-income groups as well as to locate low-income areas.

The lowest-quality housing is generally found in squatter (non-rent-paying) communities in which the threat of eviction reduces the squatter's incentive to invest in home improvements. Housing quality tends to increase among landowners, who are more likely permanent residents. A stable population requires a more permanent intervention infrastructure than does an unstable, transient, and probably lower-income squatter population liable to relocation by urban-renewal programs. In São Paulo the houses of even the lowest class seem fairly permanent, since 95 percent have covered floors.[34] Similarly, in the Cali slum Unión de Vivienda Popular 62 percent of the households owned their property, 21 percent rented, and 16 percent were nonpaying guests.[35] The houses are generally permanent because inhabitance usually in-

33. Morell and Morell, *Six Slums*, Table III-56.
34. Escola Paulista, *Estado Nutricional*, p. 27.
35. Selwyn, "Use and Nonuse," p. 137.

volves the purchase of land. In Bangkok it appears that slum dwellings, even though to a large extent occupied by squatters, are fairly well constructed: more than 90 percent of these dwellings are of wood with a metal roof.[36] Squatter housing, it must be realized, is not necessarily of low quality, though it can be expected that recently arrived squatters have lower-quality housing.

Housing-quality statistics are not generally as available as information on the use of public utilities. Where housing surveys have been undertaken, however, they are useful in locating low-income areas and classifying low-income groups. Data on squatter housing are particularly relevant in this regard. It is likely that low water and sewerage rates correlate strongly with low-quality and less permanent housing. Clustering these three indicators might pinpoint high-risk zones.

HEALTH SERVICES. The link between poor health (especially infections) and malnutrition has been clearly documented.[37] In general, more health-service facilities exist in urban areas than in rural areas, though statistics on the average availability per capita of health facilities cloak the reality of health care for the urban poor. Although preventive and basic health services may be available in the modern sector of the urban area, they are usually lacking in the slums. The sole contact of the urban poor with the health-care system may be the crowded and inadequate curative facilities of hospital outpatient departments. Slum dwellers may be unaware of the existence of health services or may be unable to use them because of geography, cost, or other barriers. The inequality and inaccessibility of health-care services is a basic problem in urban areas.

A map of preventive and curative facilities, noting existing maternal- and child-health or other nutrition-surveillance programs, and listing encounters by low-income groups for the previous year, is a useful starting point for determining service distribution. This map should also include plots of population density of the urban poor considered particularly vulnerable. The map's information should be verified by site visits.

Several possible health-service indicators exist, such as mother-child health clinics or other health and nutrition facilities for chil-

36. Morell and Morell, *Six Slums*, Table I-16.
37. Nevin S. Scrimshaw, Carl E. Taylor, and John E. Gordon, *Interactions of Nutrition and Infection*, WHO Monograph Series, no. 57 (Geneva: WHO, 1968).

dren, the number of hospital beds, clinics, or medical professionals and paraprofessionals per 1,000 inhabitants, and the percentage of the population vaccinated. Another indicator is the rate of clinic use, which shows actual coverage and therefore suggests the feasibility of using medical facilities for nutrition surveillance or as centers for education and food distribution. These ratios and indirect indicators can, however, obscure the reality of health care for low-income groups. Primary interest is in use by these vulnerable groups, not by the population in general. It may therefore be necessary to take samples in what appear to be target-group neighborhoods in order to document the actual extent of the health system. These surveys might also gather data on weaning age, breastfeeding practices, and diarrhea rate, which is both a cause and an effect of malnutrition.

EDUCATIONAL FACILITIES. Poor people often lack the skills and training necessary to improve their income. A glance at the school system tells whether it can serve as a vehicle of change. Information on school attendance is necessary if the program hopes to reach the family of the school-age child through a take-home feeding program, for example. Mapping the location of schools in low-income neighborhoods and documenting attendance rates by low-income children can indicate the feasibility of using school facilities as feeding sites, distribution points, or information centers for parents. Enrollment of squatters' children is often high, but so are dropout rates.

Given the dispersion of students in schools beyond the slum boundaries and low enrollments in the cities examined, schools appear to be a poor conduit for take-home feeding programs, but the planner should still consider them as a medium for nutrition and health messages.

Conclusions

The foregoing section has examined certain critical urban characteristics and has considered their relevance to the nutrition planner who seeks to identify target groups and to design an intervention. The utility of the various indicators is based on their availability, their predictive value as urban malnutrition correlates, and their importance to program design. Table 3-1 summarizes these indicators according to their use (intervention design or target-

Table 3-1. *Summary of Indicators of Environmental Characteristics*

Indicator	Intervention design	Target group identification	Nutritional risk predictive value	Information availability	Likely information source
Population density and growth					
Inhabitants per square kilometer	X	X	H	H	Census
Square meters of housing per resident		X	H	M	Public housing department
Annual population growth per 1,000	X[a]	X	M	H	Census, ministry of health
Migration					
Migration as percentage of total population growth		X[a]	M	M	
Migrants as percentage of low-income group	X	X[a]	M	L	Ministry of labor or welfare, universities
Elapsed time since arrival	X[a]		M	L	
Temporariness of migration	X[a]	X	M	L	
Ethnic group	X[a]		M	M	
Language	X	X	M	M	Census
Zone of origin		X	M	M	
Family size and structure					
Mean family size	X	X	H	H	Census, family planning department
Age distribution	X	X	L	H	Census
Dependency ratio		X	H	M	Ministry of labor and welfare
Single-parent households		X	M	M	Census, ministry of welfare
Family type	X		M	M	Ministry of welfare
Birth order and interval		X	H	M	Health clinics, family planning clinics, census
Maternal employment					
Percentage of working mothers	X[a]	X[a]	L	M	Ministry of labor
Hours per day away from home				L	Ministry of labor, university studies
Parent literacy					
Father	X	X	M	H	
Mother	X[a]	X	M	H	Ministry of education

34

Indicator					Responsible agency
Water					
Connections per 1,000 inhabitants	X		H	H	Public works department, utility company
Exclusive access per 1,000 inhabitants	X		H	M	
Sewerage					
Connections per 1,000 households	X		H	H	Public works department
Private W.C. per 1,000 households	X		M	M	
Electricity					
Service per 1,000 households	X[a]	X	L	H	Utility company
Television usage	X[a]			M	Television stations, advertising agencies, market research companies
Radio usage	X[a]			M	Radio stations, advertising agencies, market research companies
Housing					
Permanency (quality)	X	X	M	L	Housing department, social agencies
Nonrenters (squatters) per 1,000 households	X	X	M	L	
Transport					
Frequency of service	X[a]	X		H	Metropolitan transportation agency
Cost per trip	X[a]	X		H	Transport companies
Paved roads per square kilometer	X		M	H	Public works department
Educational services					
Schools per square kilometer	X	X		H	Ministry of education
Percentage of population attending	X	X		H	
Health services					
Beds per 1,000 inhabitants	X[a]	X	M	H	Ministry of health
Clinics per 1,000 inhabitants	X	X	M	H	
Doctors per 1,000 inhabitants	X	X	M	H	
Nurses per 1,000 inhabitants	X	X	M	H	
Paraprofessionals per 1,000 inhabitants	X[a]	X[a]	M	M	
Percentage of low-income population vaccinated		X[a]	M	H	
Clinic usage rates of low-income population per year	X[a]			M	

Note: H = high, M = medium, L = low.
a. Means highest-priority information.

35

group identification), estimated predictive value (as a target-group identifier), probable availability, and likely source.

As was mentioned previously, more field data and analysis are needed before the significance of absolute numbers or gradations of these indicators can be estimated; before, for example, the relative effect of fifty rather than five water connections per 1,000 inhabitants can be judged. Nonetheless, a study of these urban characteristics suggests which categories of information are needed for mounting urban nutrition interventions.

Informational Category 2: Economic Behavior

Because urbanites generally buy their food, their nutrient intake is largely determined by food-purchasing patterns. A low income is obviously the major constraint on food purchases, and urban poverty may worsen rather than ameliorate in the future. A 10 percent increase in India's urban poverty index has been projected.[38] Food expenditures dominate poor urbanites' incomes. For example, they absorb from one-half to two-thirds of the budgets of low-income urban dwellers in Latin America (see Table 3-2). Other influences on purchasing behavior include food habits, the processing and distribution system, price, and the urban migration and family composition factors discussed above. Data on the determinants of economic behavior are significant for the diagnosis of nutritional problems as well as for the design of the intervention.

From an economic standpoint, intervention can be achieved by both rational distribution and efficient use of nutrients. Direct food distribution or policies affecting market prices change the income-distribution pattern and therefore the availability of nutrients. In contrast, nutrition education and fortification attempt to optimize nutrient intake within existing incomes and price levels. To affect either distribution or efficiency, the planner must first understand food habits.

Food habits

The nature of the diet, food beliefs, and food practices are three particularly relevant dimensions of food habits.

38. Rashmi Mayur, "The Coming Third World Crisis: Runaway Growth of Large Cities," *The Futurist* (August 1975), p. 170.

Table 3-2. *Expenditure Profiles for Households in the Lowest-income Quartile in Latin American Cities*
(percent)

Expenditure category	Bogotá	Barranquilla	Cali	Medellín	Santiago	Quito	Guayaquil	Lima	Caracas	Maracaibo
Food and beverages	57.14	67.68	67.37	62.52	52.18	59.72	68.53	57.63	50.44	58.16
Housing[a]	22.73	14.77	14.42	19.91	23.12	19.19	16.00	14.73	23.72	19.30
Household goods and services	2.65	2.78	2.83	2.22	2.85	4.23	3.61	5.54	3.99	4.44
Clothing	4.93	3.83	4.22	2.70	9.73	8.87	4.01	5.84	5.37	2.49
Medical care	1.26	1.38	0.55	0.70	0.89	2.35	1.36	1.98	1.45	0.68
Education	4.57	2.60	1.88	2.67	0.34	0.95	1.07	1.13	1.43	0.75
Recreation and culture	1.06	1.09	1.02	0.71	2.30	0.53	1.10	2.01	2.29	1.99
Public transport	3.07	2.63	2.73	1.97	3.97	0.05	0.00	3.99	4.38	4.79
Other	2.59	3.24	4.98	6.60	4.62	4.11	4.32	7.15	6.93	7.40

Source: Philip Musgrove, *Consumer Behavior in Latin America: Income and Spending in Ten Andean Cities* (Washington, D.C.: Brookings Institution, 1978), extracted from Tables C-31 through C-40, pp. 325–34. Used by permission of the Brookings Institution.
a. Rent paid or imputed plus maintenance.

NATURE OF THE DIET. In developing countries the staples of the general population and particularly of the poor are cereals and tubers. Traditional diets, common in rural areas, are disrupted in the city, though cereals still generally represent the principal item of expenditure. In Latin American cities cereals account for about 12 percent of total expenditures at an annual income of $1,000 but drop to 5 percent at $8,000.[39] Work hours and transport limitations increase away-from-home eating and usually introduce nutritional changes. Food diversity increases, sometimes for good, sometimes for ill.

In urban areas consumption of processed and manufactured foods increases, and there appears to be a higher receptivity to food innovations. These factors may favor fortification or high-nutrition food interventions. Recent migrants, however, tend to cling to traditional foods even if they are more expensive than nutritionally equivalent alternatives in the urban marketplace.

BELIEFS ABOUT FOOD. Diets are significantly shaped by the web of belief; surrounding foods. Beliefs about the diets of infants and pregnant and lactating women are particularly strong yet are frequently ignored or underemphasized in intervention design. Many of these beliefs are not only relevant but rational—for example, the common belief that food intake during the third trimester of pregnancy should be reduced. This practice tends to produce low-birth-weight (and, therefore, nutritionally vulnerable) babies, but it may also reduce birth complications that obtain when a large baby is born to a small mother.

Of particular concern are attitudes and practices regarding breastfeeding and weaning. An examination of data on country and city attitudes reveals a decline in the incidence and duration of breastfeeding in urban areas.[40] In Bangkok slums one-fourth of the children received only canned milk from birth, while in the rural areas breastfeeding is nearly universal.[41] The apparent rea-

39. Musgrove, *Consumer Behavior*, p. 162.

40. Dana Raphael, "The Role of Breastfeeding in a Bottle-Oriented World," *Ecology of Food and Nutrition*, vol. 2 (1973), p. 121. Joe D. Wray, "Breastfeeding and the Urban Poor of the Third World" (paper presented at the American Academy of Arts and Sciences Annual Meeting, February 21, 1976). For a general survey of breastfeeding and nutrition, see D. B. Jelliffe and E. F. P. Jelliffe, *Human Milk in the Modern World* (Oxford: Oxford University Press, 1978).

41. Morell and Morell, *Six Slums*, p. 46.

sons for this decline are insufficient milk, the mother's work, and higher status associated with bottle feeding. Breastfeeding can be encouraged through nutrition education or child-care facilities at work locations for working mothers, but the increase in alternative infant feeding practices will not easily be reversed. Accordingly, effort is needed to ensure that alternative foods are reasonably priced and that mothers are taught their proper, hygienic use.

Although prolonged breastfeeding is desirable, late introduction and insufficient quantities of supplemental foods for the weanling are the most common causes of infant malnutrition. Extended breastfeeding without adequate supplementation seems a more predominant problem in rural areas but is still significant in urban areas. Beliefs largely determine what foods are given to the infant and when, though cost and availability are also relevant factors. In many cities appropriate weaning foods at affordable prices are not available, but new foods and price subsidies might help solve this problem. In other instances, current weaning foods such as cornstarch are nutritionally deficient and could be improved with other cheap foods such as oil, vegetables, and rice. Nutrition education is appropriate for getting mothers to make these additions to their children's diet.

During illness food taboos come into play. For example, during bouts of infant diarrhea or febrile illness foods are frequently withheld; this results in starving the child or prolonging and aggravating the illness. Changing prices will not modify this behavior; communication between nutrition educators and health interventionists is required. Physicians and other health professionals generally receive inadequate training in nutrition and consequently may actually disseminate misinformation about nutrition and food habits.

Religious and cultural beliefs can proscribe and prescribe foods both periodically, as in periods of fasting, and permanently, as in vegetarianism.

FOOD PRACTICES. Urban work requirements affect meal patterns among other food practices. In urban areas more meals are eaten out because of work schedules, and knowing which meals play the dominant nutritional role can help planners tailor interventions to fit the working mother's schedule.

Food distribution within the family determines the nutritional well-being of individuals targeted for help. In many cultures adult male heads of household seem to have first access to family food. Data on this practice, though scarce, are highly relevant to intervention design, for the practice can perhaps be influenced by nutrition education.

Cooking facilities and hence food preparation differ widely in urban and rural areas. Since preparation practices such as fuel conservation and cooking techniques affect nutrition, they are relevant to fortification, price interventions, and nutrition education. Storage and preparation of water for consumption and cleaning are also relevant.

Food-processing and -distribution system

The major dimensions of the processing and distribution system that merit examination in choosing an effective intervention are food purchasing, the use of retail outlets, and the food marketing structure.

Constraints on cash flow and storage facilities in urban areas necessitate small and frequent purchases. This practice leads to patronage of nearby, small, low-income retail stores that often extend informal credit and are open long hours. In some regions those stores tend to offer a narrow product line and carry poor items, are inefficient, and charge high prices. In other areas, however, small stores are highly competitive. The how, when, and where must be addressed in considering alternative distribution systems, such as government fair-price shops, or in selecting existing private outlets to reach target groups.

The structure of wholesale food distribution channels should also be examined. Wholesale storage and distribution facilities in urban areas are frequently defective, unhygienic, and wasteful, occasioning food losses that push up costs for the retail consumer. Storage inadequacies in the home can also lead to food contamination and loss. The distribution system may be so highly fragmented that many middlemen intervene before products reach the consumer, a characteristic that increases distribution costs and margins. Thus, market locations, access to transport, and business hours are important details to examine. Finally, a small number of wholesalers may manipulate prices, and planners should try to ascertain if public regulation is needed in this area.

Food processing should be examined for hygiene and to detect nutritionally deleterious practices such as the possible loss of nutrients. Promotional techniques for commercial foods such as infant formulas may only worsen the nutritional status of vulnerable groups. Governments and commercial firms should reexamine the implications of promotional activities.

Food demand

The great majority get their food through the family, and, at least in urban areas, most of that food is obtained in the market. To understand a family's food-purchasing behavior, demand can be estimated relative to family income, prices of food and nonfood items, and factors such as family size, composition, and ethnic allegiance that affect preference for particular foodstuffs. The nutritional adequacy of consumption depends on the quality and quantity of food and on the ways in which it is stored, prepared, and served. It is, however, misleading to consider diet only in its adequacy for a family, because the distribution of food among family members determines individual intake more precisely. Still, most feasible programs for large-scale nutritional intervention have to work indirectly through the family. Therefore, to estimate the likely effect of a program on nutritionally deficient groups, its effect on family decisionmaking must first be considered. It is also important to understand how each nutrition intervention is likely to affect individuals within families.

PROGRAMS FOR DISTRIBUTING FOOD. Programs that subsidize or distribute foodstuffs improve the quantity and quality of nutrients families obtain. With respect to subsidy or feeding programs that lower the price of particular foods or give them away, it is important to identify the precise pattern of substitution effects. Even though more subsidized food will be purchased or donated food consumed, they will partially supplant other foodstuffs, and the net nutritional effect will generally be less than estimated by direct price elasticities. Furthermore, in the case of staples, lower prices or free foods may primarily represent an income subsidy that may divert purchasing power to nonfood items or to less nutritious foods such as soft drinks. Special nutrient-dense foods tailored to the needs of particular target groups (for example, weaning foods for children under 2) may reduce the substitution and intrafamilial dilution effects.

In examining price subsidy or donated food it must be recognized that these schemes, if not properly designed, can result in lower farmer prices. If farm prices drop, production may fall and the nutritional effect of the subsidy can be lost, since the resultant scarcity might increase prices beyond the value of the subsidy.

REDISTRIBUTION OF INCOME. Programs such as ration shops or food coupons that affect income directly through subsidy also affect nutritional status to the extent that the family buys more and better food, which is distributed among family members with unfilled nutritional needs.

FORTIFICATION. This intervention changes the nutritional content of certain mass-consumed foods—for example, by adding iodine to salt or vitamin A to sugar. The effect of fortification depends on the extent to which fortified foods are purchased or otherwise obtained by the family, are prepared in ways which do not degrade the nutrients, and are available to the family members deficient in the nutritional elements supplied.

EDUCATION IN NUTRITION. Such education can have effect in at least four ways: by engendering preference for food over nonfood items; by increasing awareness of the value of nutrients which leads, it is hoped, to favoring more nutritious foods; by imparting knowledge of how to store and prepare foods to increase their nutritional content; and—perhaps of greatest importance—by providing information about the nutritional needs of children and pregnant women that affects the intrafamilial distribution of food. Education is effective, however, only if it changes food consumption for the better.

It is clear in the foregoing consideration that information on price, income, and family composition is indispensable in estimating the possible effect of interventions, particularly of the first three mentioned above. Furthermore, information on intrafamilial distribution of food is required to identify nutritionally disadvantaged groups and to estimate how programs will affect individual consumption.

Fortunately, a usable data source, the household expenditure survey commonly conducted to estimate the cost-of-living index, exists in many countries. Most such surveys divide food into specific categories, from which it is possible to estimate the food's nutritional content. Furthermore, most of these studies provide information on the number, sex, and age of household members. These data provide a basis for estimating demand elasticities and the probable effects of various interventions in family food consumption. Some effort has been made to develop econometric models that would permit a more precise assessment of target groups' economic behavior.[42]

Informational Category 3: Nutritional Status

Although examination of urban environmental characteristics and economic behavior factors can go a long way toward identifying groups at risk, the design of intervention programs requires the use of even more precise instruments to specify the scope and nature of the deficiencies to be combatted. This section will contain discussion of information provided by direct and indirect indicators.

Direct indicators

Direct indicators include anthropometry and clinical and biochemical assessment. Nutritional anthropometry measures the variations in physical dimension and gross composition of the human body at different ages and varying states of nutrition. Of the direct methodologies, it is the most widely used and studied and the least expensive. For adults, however, the only commonly used form of anthropometry is measurement of weight gain in pregnant women.

ANTHROPOMETRY. Anthropometric measurements of height and weight are used to assess the pattern of growth in children. Retarded growth is the earliest and most sensitive indicator of malnutrition among children.

A weight-for-age ratio is derived by taking a child's weight and dividing it by the 50th percentile weight of well-nourished children of the same age. It is a particularly useful measurement for children under the age of 2 years, in whom a weight deficit for any reason signifies a failure to grow adequately. According to the Gomez

42. Shlomo Reutlinger and Marcelo Selowsky, *Malnutrition and Poverty: Magnitude and Policy Options*, World Bank Staff Occasional Papers, no. 23 (Baltimore: Johns Hopkins University Press, 1976), pp. 53–82; Dave Wheeler and others, in "Urban Malnutrition: Problem Assessment and Intervention Guidelines" (a report to the World Bank, September 1976), a restricted-circulation document, pp. 98–106, 227–67.

Table 3-3. *Simplified Four-cell Classification of Nutritional Status,
by Height for Age and Weight for Height*

Height for age[a] \ *Weight for height*[a]	*Normal (95+)*	*Mild (90–94)*	*Moderate (85–89)*	*Severe (<85)*
Normal (90+) Mild (80–89)	Normal to mild		Stunting	
Moderate (70–79) Severe (70)	Wasting		Stunting and wasting	

Source: Adapted from J. C. Waterlow, "Classification and Definition of Protein-Calorie Malnutrition," *British Medical Journal,* no. 3 (1972), p. 566. Used by permission of the British Medical Association.

a. Percentage of median.

classification, a quotient of less than 60 percent of weight for age is third-degree malnutrition, 60 percent to 74 percent is second-degree, 75 percent to 90 percent is first-degree, and above 90 percent is normal.[43] The weight-for-age ratio has also been shown to have predictive value in identifying immunologic deficit and therefore susceptibility to infections in a malnourished child.[44] Thus, anthropometric measurements may also partially predict the relative vulnerability of malnourished groups to various infectious diseases.

The height-for-age ratio is found by dividing the actual height by the 50th-percentile height of well-nourished children of the same age. The weight-for-height ratio is the actual weight divided by the 50th-percentile weight of children of the same height. Height for age and weight for height are useful measurements because they distinguish between acute and chronic malnutrition. The best way of combining these measurements is shown in Table 3-3.

Deficit in linear growth, defined as the condition of being under 90 percent of the reference median height for one's age, suggests past chronic undernutrition and is termed "stunting." Current acute, short-duration undernutrition, termed "wasting," is recent weight loss in which the individual's weight-for-height ratio is under 80 percent of the reference median. A child simultaneously scoring under 80 percent in the weight-for-height ratio and under

43. F. Gomez and others, "Mortality in Second- and Third-Degree Malnutrition," *Journal of Tropical Pediatrics,* vol. 2, no. 2, pp. 77–83.

44. V. Reddy and others, "Functional Significance of Growth Retardation in Malnutrition," *American Journal of Clinical Nutrition,* vol. 29 (January 1976), pp. 3–7.

90 percent in the height-for-age ratio is classified as suffering concurrent wasting and stunting.

With no local standards, common practice is to use the Harvard standards or the National Academy of Sciences standards[45] because the probable degrees of genetic effect on the height- and weight-for-age ratios are not more than 3 and 6 percent, respectively, among children from different ethnic backgrounds but of similar social class. By contrast, differences between malnourished and well-nourished children of the same ethnic background approach 12 percent for height and 30 percent for weight.

Errors in anthropometric measurements can occur. In many cultures no record is kept of children's exact ages, which must be estimated from a local events calendar; births may be registered, but when the child is several weeks or even months old. The length of infants under 2 is measured while they are lying down and will be inaccurate unless two persons help in the measurement, making sure that both head and feet are touching surfaces perpendicular to the surface on which the child lies. And spring scales lose accuracy over time.

Alternatively, arm or thigh circumferences can be used. These are more simply obtained, requiring only tape and causing no discomfort to the child, but they are slightly less accurate than other anthropometric measurements and lose anthropometry's advantage of being translatable into growth charts that mothers can understand and maintain—a progressive surveillance tool and means of eliciting active community participation.[46]

---

45. See, respectively, V. C. Vaughan, "Growth and Development in the Infant and Child," in *Textbook of Pediatrics,* 8th ed., ed. W. E. Nelson (Philadelphia: W. B. Saunders, 1964) and Food and Nutrition Board, "Mean Heights and Weights and Recommended Energy Intakes" (table), in *Recommended Dietary Allowances,* 9th ed. (Washington, D.C.: National Academy of Sciences, forthcoming).

46. E. F. P. Jelliffe and D. B. Jelliffe, "The Arm Circumference as a Public Health Index of Protein-Calorie Malnutrition of Early Childhood," and H. J. L. Burgess and A. P. Burgess, "A Modified Standard for Mid-Upper Arm Circumference in Young Children," both in *Journal of Tropical Pediatrics,* no. 15 (December 1969); Marian Zeitlin, "Reference Standards for Maximum Thigh Circumference, 0–5 Years; Thigh Circumference—An Age-Independent Screening Index for Preschool Nutrition Interventions" (Ph.D. dissertation, Massachusetts Institute of Technology, Cambridge, Mass., 1977); and Marian Zeitlin and James Austin, "Impediments and Requirements of Nutrition Evaluation" (paper presented at the International Nutrition Congress, Rio de Janeiro, August 1978).

CLINICAL ASSESSMENT. Clinical assessment of malnutrition involves the examination of physical changes that can be seen or felt in the superficial skin tissues. The problem with clinical assessment as a tool in diagnosing malnutrition is that the overwhelming majority of nutritional deficiencies are subclinical. When 50 percent of a population of children are moderately to severely malnourished, perhaps fewer than 1 percent show clinical symptoms. Malnutrition exists, but these measuring instruments are not sufficiently sensitive to detect them. Thus, the utility of clinical assessment alone in the diagnosis of malnutrition is negligible. After persons who assess growth are taught to recognize clinical symptoms, however, they can detect a small but important number of cases that will provide valuable insight into specific deficiency patterns such as pellagra, beriberi, vitamin A deficiency, or rickets.

BIOCHEMICAL ASSESSMENT. Biochemical assessment examines samples of a variety of bodily fluids (urine, blood) for a biochemical estimate of nutritional significance. A wide variety of biochemical tests are available and are nutrient specific for vitamin A, the B-complex, calcium, folate, vitamin C, iron, vitamin B-12, protein, and trace minerals. Because these tests are nutrient specific, they can generate information on the prevalence of general nutrient deficits in the population.

Nevertheless, biochemical evaluations are good only as ancillary tools because their expense, relative to anthropometry, is generally prohibitive for large-scale surveys. Small-scale studies are useful to document a hypothesis that the community suffers from a specific nutrient deficit. Biochemical evaluations of interventions are valuable, for they can register changes in nutritional status not identifiable by other means.

Indirect indicators

Indirect indicators are surrogate measures of nutritional status. They include food balance sheets, vital statistics, and food-consumption surveys. Food balance sheets indicate food availability in a country over a one-year period. Since the data are gross estimates of per capita caloric supplies, they do not reveal distributional inequities and thus are of limited value in problem diagnosis.

Malnutrition influences morbidity, maternal and perinatal mortality rates, and life expectancy for those suffering from various diseases. Therefore, nutritionists consider vital statistics as indirect indicators of nutritional status. High 1- to 4-year-old mortality is a strong malnutrition correlate; deathrates of over 10 per 1,000 of the 1-to-4 population are indicative of widespread PCM. High infant mortality rates (greater than 70 deaths per 1,000 live births) are similarly indicative, and such data are generally available. Birth weights of newborns can be used as an indirect measure of maternal nutritional status, because chronic malnutrition of the mother or severe caloric deficiency during pregnancy reduces the birth weight and decreases body length and head circumference of full-term infants. Birth weight appears to be a partial predictor of survival during the first year of life.

Food-consumption surveys provide information on dietary intake. Individual dietary surveys of preschool and of pregnant and lactating groups over twenty-four hours provide essential information, particularly on nutrient deficits, which forms the basis for designing interventions to deliver needed nutrients. These surveys are subject to inaccuracies because of poor memory, observer bias, and atypical sampling of diet. Refinement can be achieved through food weighing and surveys of the same family over several days.[47] Household consumption surveys are more available and are useful in economic analysis, although they fail to indicate the nutritional intake of malnourished family members, since they do not consider absorption, body nutrient stores, and genetic variation.

The cost of carrying out nutritional status surveys can vary considerably, depending on their scope and design. Anthropometric surveys can be reasonably economical and accurate. Field surveys that included anthropometry and selected biochemical tests have been conducted in several developing countries at a cost of approximately $15 a child for a sample of 5,000 children, over a data collection and analysis period of six to twelve months. This cost could probably be reduced to about $2 a child by measuring weight only, by limiting the sample to children under 3 years old, and by using cluster-sampling techniques from blocks or streets representative of identified urban slum areas. The turnaround period for these data would probably be between one and three months. Such sur-

47. G. C. Hagen and others, "Comparison of Dietary History and Seven-Day Record with 24-Hour Recall," *Massachusetts Experiment Station Bulletin 469* (1952), pp. 31–38; and Ruth L. Pike and Myrtle Brown, *Nutrition, An Integrated Approach* (New York: John Wiley and Sons, 1975), pp. 937–43.

veys are an essential part of project design, since they provide a basic reference against which subsequent project evaluations can be compared.

Both direct and indirect indicators can identify individuals or subgroups of the population in danger of nutritional deficiency. Because it is clear that all indicators provide certain useful information, a nutrition planner's starting point for assessing nutritional status should be an examination of existing data, which may include many of the indicators mentioned. Table 3-4, presented as a summary guide for data interpretation, indicates the relevant direct and indirect indicators for each group and the approximate level at which significant risk may occur.

To judge more precisely the utility of existing data and to determine what additional nutritional status data should be ascertained, the planner must assess the relative merits of the various indicators.

Table 3-4. *Guidelines for Interpretation of Data on Nutritional Status*

Type of data	Risk level	Data source
Infants under 1 year		
Direct indicators		
Anthropometry		
Birth weight	Under 2.2 kilograms	Hospitals, mother-
Weight for age	Gomez standards: any 2–3d degree malnutrition	child health clinics, bureau of health, anthropometric studies
Height for age	WHO criteria	
Weight for height	WHO criteria	
Indirect indicators		
Vital statistics		
Perinatal mortality	35 per 1,000 live births	Ministry of health
Neonatal mortality	70 per 1,000 live births	
Cause of death	20 percent due to malnutrition	
Incidence of infectious disease	Epidemic	
Dietary studies/ infant feeding practices		
Weaning diet	Under 3 months	Dietary studies
Solid introduction	Introduction over 6 months	
Breastfeeding practices	Decline in breastfeeding	
Preparation of weaning foods	Dilution of formula or dry mixes	

Table 3-4 *(continued)*

Type of data	Risk level	Data source
	Infants from 1 to 5 years	
Direct indicators		
Anthropometry		
Weight for age	Gomez classification: any 2–3d degree malnutri- tion	Small anthropometric studies
Height for age	WHO standards	
Weight for height	WHO standards	
Indirect indicators		
Vital statistics		
1 to 4 year mortality	70 per 1,000 live births	Ministry of health,
Incidence of infectious disease	Epidemic, diarrhea rate	expert opinion, hospi- tals, mother-child
Cause of death	20 percent malnutrition- related	health clinics
Dietary studies		
Pattern of intrafamilial food consumption	Unequal portion given to child when considering requirements	Survey
	Pregnant women	
Direct indicators		
Anthropometry		
Weight gain	Under 25 pounds	Clinics, hospitals, ex- pert opinion, surveys
Clinical		
Anemia	12 milligrams per 100 milliliters hemogloblin	
Parasitism		
Indirect indicators		
Vital statistics		
Maternal mortality	1.0 per 100	Ministry of health
Abortions		
Number of pregnancies		
Dietary studies		
Food taboos		Expert opinion,
Food beliefs		surveys
Feeding practices		

Adults

The range of indicators to be used with adults are considered by Derrick B. Jelliffe in *Assessment of Nutrition Status in the Community* (Geneva: WHO, 1966). Aside from general vital and health statistics, evaluation of status in the adult will necessitate clinical and biochemical evaluations.

Note: Data should be stratified by urban and rural areas. Within cities, this stratification can be done by zone to illuminate any differences in locality of malnutrition that may be masked by grouping data.

For example, Table 3-5 presents a matrix comparison of the indicators against the criteria of accuracy, cost, skill, and time. The assessments in the table depend on subjective judgment and should be viewed with caution. Even the reliability of vital statistics can vary considerably from country to country.

Among the direct indicators, anthropometry, and among the indirect indicators, vital statistics, do the best job of balancing the four criteria, but all the indicators in the table can serve the planner's various purposes. To start with, all available findings for any of the indicators should be used, and additional data should be gathered depending on the planner's objectives, financial resources, and time available. As the planning process of nutrition intervention proceeds, additional information and greater accuracy become necessary. For example, a suspicion that a serious nutritional problem exists in a certain area might emerge from a review of vital statistics or by listening to the opinions of local experts. Estimating the magnitude and severity of the problem might require examining individual or household surveys and anthropometric data. Designing an actual intervention will necessitate dietary studies of food patterns and nutritional deficits. Similarly, bio-

Table 3-5. *Evaluation of Methodologies for Direct and Indirect Assessment*

	Criteria			
Indicator	*Accuracy*	*Cost*	*Skill*	*Time*
Direct				
Anthropometry	H	M	L	L
Clinical	M	M	H	H
Biochemical	H	H	H	L
Indirect				
Individual survey				
24-hour recall	M	M	M	L
Food diary	M	L	M	L
Diet history	M	M	M	M
Weighed food intake	H	H	H	H
Household survey				
Food account	L	L	M	M
Food list	M	L	M	M
Food record	M	M	M	M
Weighed consumption	H	H	H	H
Vital statistics	M	L	L	L
Food balance sheets	L	L	L	L

Note: H = High; M = Medium; L = Low.

Table 3-6. *Types of Information Indicating Nutritional Status Used in Nutrition Planning*

Planning	Food balance sheet	Vital statistics	Expert opinion[a]	Household expenditure surveys	Anthropometry	Dietary studies of the target group	Biochemical and clinical data
Macro level							
Problem diagnosis	X	X					
Micro level							
Problem diagnosis		X	X	X	X[b]		
Selection and development of interventions			X	X	X	X	X
Monitoring and evaluation		X		X	X	X	X

a. Includes health, socioeconomic and political environment, dietary practices, staples, beliefs and taboos, marketing and food-distribution mechanisms, cultural and anthropological characteristics.

b. Includes screening to identify target groups.

chemical data might then be needed to ascertain the severity of certain micronutrient deficiencies. Table 3-6 illustrates this process of sequential and multiple use of indicators.[48]

48. See also Table 3-1, which, in analogous fashion, indicates the use of urban environmental characteristics to identify target groups.

4

The Design of the Intervention

The foregoing information on urban environmental characteristics, economic behavior, and nutritional status forms the basis for the definition of the problem, identification of the target group, and design of the intervention. Nine direct nutrition interventions can be directed toward target groups among the urban malnourished: nutrition education, on-site feeding, take-home feeding, nutrient-dense foods, ration shops, food coupons, fortification, direct nutrient dosage, and food processing and marketing.

In addition to these direct nutrition interventions, there are several indirect forms of intervention that, by dealing primarily with health, water and sanitation, and family planning, also clearly influence the nutritional well-being of target groups. Although this section focuses principally on direct approaches, ancillary interventions will also be considered in the interest of integrating direct and indirect nutrition programs. Far from being ignored, such integration is strongly recommended. A thorough understanding of direct programs will facilitate complementary applications of both direct and indirect interventions.

Available intervention options employed either singly or together address different causes underlying malnutrition. Table 4-1 presents a matrix illustrating the relations between the causes of malnutrition and various nutrition interventions. Clearly, the logical starting point for nutrition programming is the isolation of the causes to be addressed. Table 4-1 also shows that some causes may require the simultaneous application of different interventions.

Note: The section "Integrated Approaches," below, benefited particularly from research carried out by Rhonda Sarnoff.

Table 4-1. *Cause of Malnutrition and Appropriate Nutrition Intervention*

Intervention	Knowledge, belief	Intra-familial food distribution	Food-type availability	Food quality	Food-system inefficiency	Food-system conduct	Income level
				Cause			
Nutrition education	X	X					
On-site feeding		X					X
Take-home feeding							X
Nutrient-dense foods			X	X			
Ration shops							X
Food coupons							X
Fortification			X	X			
Direct nutrient dosage			X	X			
Food processing and marketing					X	X	

This section will deal with major design considerations for each program option.

Although each nutrition intervention has a distinctive design, all share common goals. First, all interventions should be directed toward the most vulnerable groups—which, as indicated earlier, tend to be children under 3 and pregnant and lactating women. Information on exactly who they are, where they are located, what their deficiencies are, and how they are best reached is derived from the information sources examined in the previous chapter. Second, interventions should economize on scarce human and financial resources. Third, and perhaps most important, they should strive to involve their beneficiaries as much as possible in the program's design and operation.

Nutrition Education

Where erroneous beliefs or ignorance lead to poor use of nutrient resources, nutrition education is appropriate. If nutrient deficiencies exist throughout all income levels or if, despite adequate nourishment for the aggregate family, the preschooler or the pregnant or lactating mother suffers from malnutrition, nutrition education is indicated. For example, a study in India of two castes concluded that "among Jats, beliefs clearly are most important, suggesting that interventions solely designed to affect these belief patterns might have significant effects on food intake."[1]

The design of the intervention involves two main components: development of the message and selection of the media to be used.

Development of the message

The vital first step to designing specific messages is to select the subjects for education, such as breastfeeding, boiling of water, or the use of weaning food. Around these subjects a series of messages can be built whose content will be influenced by the communications vehicle selected. For example, the face-to-face approach permits longer messages and personal interaction, whereas mass communication is generally characterized by shorter messages without the opportunity for interaction except among listeners. In both cases, certain general guidelines apply. First, the message should be based on a thorough documentation of the nature of the harmful practice and its causes. The examination should be sensitive to the social and economic forces dictating this behavior. For example, decreased breastfeeding is a trend in urban areas closely associated with adverse nutritional status, but a message urging mothers to breastfeed might be ineffectual if the underlying reason for their seeking alternatives is their having to work. In this case, efforts to alter workplace arrangements to facilitate child care and continued breastfeeding might be more effective. The research underlying the message should also identify precisely who makes the operative decision (see chapter 3, the subsection "Family size and structure"). Pregnant women who ought, for instance, to increase their assimilation of available but taboo proteins might best be reached indirectly through their mothers or local authority figures, such as midwives and religious or community leaders.

A second general rule for the content of a message is to make it

1. F. James Levinson, *Morinda: An Economic Analysis of Malnutrition among Young Children in Rural India* (Cambridge, Mass.: Cornell/Massachusetts Institute of Technology International Nutrition Policy Series, 1974), p. 64.

short, simple, and sustained. The target group generally has had limited education, and its capacity for absorption is further restricted by the plethora of information in urban areas. The shorter and more intelligible the message, the greater the likelihood of its being subsequently spread by the free word-of-mouth system. The message must be disseminated with sufficient frequency and duration to make a lasting impression on the audience, although excessive frequency can lead to message fatigue and to lower retention and motivation.

The third consideration is that the message suggest a practical course of action. The behavior change being sought—and this is the essence of education interventions—must be feasible. For example, to urge the use of weaning foods is meaningless unless such products, or at least suitable ingredients, exist in the market and are cheap enough for the target group. Food preparation demonstrations should use only locally available ingredients and typical cooking utensils and facilities.

Selection of the media

The basic alternatives are face-to-face and mass-media communications. Each has several permutations, such as group discussions, individual counseling, nutrition surveillance, radio, television, films, printed material, and posters. The choice between the alternatives depends on relative coverage, cost, and effect on behavior modification, but the two approaches should not be thought of as mutually exclusive. On the contrary, they can be reinforcing and complementary. The mass media generally offer broader coverage at lower cost, and they can be particularly effective in creating awareness and even increasing knowledge. Where the desired behavior change is relatively minor, mass media may be quite effective, but where traditional behavior is more ingrained and its modification might have undesirable consequences, it may be necessary to supplement the media with personal contact.

Coverage by mass media can be estimated by determining how many radios are within broadcast range, the size of the listening audience, and the time of day the message will be broadcast. For face-to-face persuasion, calculation of the coverage involves the disseminator-to-audience ratio, the duration of the talk, and the time spent in travel. The personal approach is more economically feasible in urban than in rural areas because of the easier accessibility and high density of the target group. The place of the education intervention can vary, but clinics and feeding sites are often advantageous because their health services or food attract a captive audience.

Personnel requirements

The mass-media approach requires fewer people but greater skills. Message design calls for consumer research; production demands professional audiovisual aids; dissemination requires media specialists. In contrast, face-to-face nutrition education can be carried out by lay personnel after a month or two of training. This training should, however, be repeated perhaps every six months to reinforce and expand the educators' knowledge. The audiovisual materials used either in mass-media or personal approaches can be produced at a national center. A national center for nutrition and health education materials can be the most economical means of making available scarce audiovisual equipment and professional skills and is a way of achieving uniformity and complementarity among the institutions engaged in nutrition education. The advice and direct help of private media firms can ensure the proper execution of such undertakings.

A paucity of information makes it impossible to form a conclusive judgment about the relative effectiveness of these two educational approaches. Evaluations of nutrition programs to date have measured expansion of knowledge but have seldom documented changes in practice and improved nutritional status. Behavior modification can generally be translated into incremental nutrient consumption and thus be compared to other interventions. In making such comparisons, however, it should be recognized that education has potentially a multiplier effect that increases coverage at little or no additional cost. First, the original message can reach a broader audience by word of mouth. Second, the behavior change, if permanent, affects the health of present and future generations. In this sense, nutrition education is analogous to immunization. Experience, however, unfortunately suggests that knowledge retention and especially permanent behavior modification are difficult to attain. Consequently, it is generally necessary to view education intervention as a continuing effort in which subsequent rounds will positively reinforce new behavior and perhaps effect incremental improvements.

On-site Feeding

On-site feeding for preschoolers—preferably under 3 years old—may be appropriate where income constraints or intrafamilial food distribution patterns prevent adequate child nutrition. Supplemental feeding (on-site or take-home) can also be viewed as a means of redressing malnutrition from other causes. For example, by attracting others, food can be used to begin the nutritional education of parents, to deal with adult health problems, or to stimulate children. Feeding alone addresses the symptom, not the cause. In the short run, its rationale derives from justice and humanitarian considerations, but it is not a long-run solution unless it forms part of a larger socioeconomic intervention.

The design of the on-site feeding intervention should deal with four basic aspects: location, participation, food logistics, and food type.

Location

The first design issue concerns the location of the feeding sites, and here two criteria are applicable: accessibility and capital requirements. The planners want to maximize the former and minimize the latter. From the urban environment information in chapter 3, they can locate the target groups. They should then select feeding centers within walking distance of their homes or easily accessible by public transport. Travel time and cost should be verified. Clinics, schools, churches, and day-care centers are logical sites because they are based on the existing infrastructure and can simultaneously facilitate the nutritional education of mothers, if desired. Although in some instances new centers will have to be organized, it will usually be possible to recondition existing facilities rather than build entirely new ones. New constructions are justified only if they can be used for other purposes throughout the day.

Participation

The issue of who should participate in the feeding program must be related to the definition of the target group. Participation can be limited to those who have been individually certified as suffering a determined degree of malnutrition. The extreme form of this approach is to run nutrition rehabilitation centers that intern severely malnourished children and restore them to health by intensive feeding and clinical treatment. Domiciliary treatment, rather than interning, is receiving increased attention and seems cheaper and more effective in preventing relapse.[2] A more preventive approach that avoids the cost of assessing individual participants' status is to declare an entire slum neighborhood at risk. The malnutrition correlates in chapter 3 can be of use in this approach. All children under 3 and pregnant and lactating women from that area would be eligible, but because it may be difficult for parents to bring only their children under 3, older siblings might also have to be fed.

The balance between prevention and cure and how strictly age limits are observed depend on the availability of resources and on the tradeoff between excess coverage and the cost of identifying and controlling the target group. Regardless of the approach, all activities should make potential beneficiaries aware of the program and motivate them to participate. To achieve this goal, other local institutions such as clinics, schools, churches, and community groups can be enlisted in the conception, design, and management of the program. Once the program is operating, word of mouth will help it along.

A final consideration is payment by the beneficiaries. It may be feasible to ask program participants to pay something in cash or in kind to help finance the feeding program. But where the income constraint is severe, this policy will be counterproductive, since it will occasion a reduction in the child's allocation of food at home. Some substitution effect appears likely in any case. For on-site feeding programs in Costa Rica and India the extent of substitution was estimated at 37 percent and 53 percent, respectively.[3] It may be more desirable to receive the parent's contribution in the form of assisting or supervising activities at the site. This approach would enhance community participation, commitment, and responsibility in the nutrition improvement program.

Logistics

The logistics of feeding programs involve both food preparation and delivery. Preparation can take place either on site or at a cen-

2. R. D. Khare, P. M. Shah, and A. R. Junnarkar, "Management of Kwashiorkor in Its Milieu: A Follow-up for Fifteen Months," *Indian Journal of Medical Research*, vol. 64, no. 8 (1976), pp. 1119–27.

3. M. A. Anderson, CARE *Preschool Nutrition Project, Phase II Report* (New York, 1977), pp. 40–46.

tralized kitchen. In urban areas with several different feeding sites, there is a strong argument for centralized preparation. Since mass feeding lends itself to economies of scale in food preparation, a central kitchen not only permits more efficient cooking and economizes on scarce managerial resources, but also allows greater flexibility in site selection. By standardizing the nutrient package, the central kitchen increases quality control, which is particularly important for preschoolers with their greater susceptibility to gastronomic disturbance. Finally, centralized procurement can achieve economies by purchasing in volume and can reduce handling losses and storage costs.

Sometimes it is possible and desirable to have the central kitchen related to, or operated by, the local food-technology and nutrition institute. The institute's facilities would be better used and its training opportunities increased. The institute might even enjoy new food development possibilities.

The obvious drawback to centralization is the need for a good transport system. This system requires an investment in storage containers and probably small trucks equipped to prevent microbial contamination during transport. Government food marketing agencies may be able to provide such services through the use of existing logistics facilities. Competent administrators are essential to efficient and effective programming of logistics as well as to supervision of food preparation. Nutritionists and food technologists will be required in the menu planning and processing operations. A link with the local nutrition institute could also be of help in this respect.

Food types

The foods used in the centers should be tested for organoleptic acceptability, since even "captive consumers" at a feeding site will not necessarily eat unappetizing foods. A varied menu may enhance acceptability, as will nutrient-dense food of reduced bulk. Basic grains in their traditional form do not meet this criterion. Finally, the quantity and nutrient composition of the food should be appropriate to the type and extent of nutrient deficits in the target group. The portion of the deficits to be filled will depend on available resources. Although research data on functional impairment are not conclusive, it appears more advisable to meet, say, 80 percent of recommended requirements for many people than to nourish fewer people completely.

A final consideration about on-site feeding and the products selected is the program's effect on the supply of these products. An adequate supply should be verified beforehand, and the program's effect on the market price of these products should be estimated. If supply is tight, added demand will push prices up and hurt other consumers. While price pressure can be alleviated by imports, this strategy has the disadvantage of using up generally scarce foreign exchange. Food-aid imports might ease this situation, but such assistance should generally be viewed as a means of buying time until local production expands.[4] Furthermore, if the type of food is not locally available, its educational value is lost and the beneficiaries' dependence on the program is accentuated to the detriment of their self-reliance.

Take-home Feeding

The take-home alternative may be appropriate where there is income constraint, where particular nutritional supplements—especially weaning foods—are needed, and where on-site feeding facilities are lacking. Take-home programs, like on-site operations, can be examined according to participation, location, food logistics, and food type and quantity. A major problem to be considered in this form of intervention is sharing the ration among other family members once it is taken home. Program design is therefore of utmost importance, especially in regard to quantity and type of food.

Participation

Participants in a take-home program should be selected according to the same criteria cited above for on-site feeding. In addition, however, more direct participation by pregnant and lactating women is necessary. This is difficult to achieve unless a special motivational effort is mounted. Contacting these women at clinics, hospi-

---

4. Simon Maxwell, "Food Aid for Supplementary Feeding Programmes—An Analysis," *Food Policy*, vol. 3, no. 4 (November 1978), pp. 289–98; James Austin and Mitchell Wallerstein, "Reformulating U.S. Food Aid Policy for Development," *World Development*, vol. 7 (July-August 1979).

tal delivery rooms, or through midwives is a good starting point. Using volunteer or part-time health workers from the communities can facilitate this outreach task.

Location and logistics

Considerations of location and food logistics are closely allied in a take-home program. Location refers to the point at which the food is distributed. As with on-site programs, the location should be relatively accessible to the target group, but proximity may be less important because the beneficiary can make periodic pickups every two weeks instead of coming by every day. The larger the take-home ration, however, the shorter should be the distance for carrying the burden. Distribution points should be located at existing facilities such as clinics, churches, community organizations, or schools. Schoolchildren might actually carry the food home from a school—if there are school-age children in the target-group families and their school attendance is high (see chapter 3, the subsection "Physical and institutional environment").

The absence of cooking and feeding functions simplifies the logistical demands of the take-home program. The task consists primarily in the delivery of a few products and in inventory management. Considerable care must be taken to ensure that storage containers and centers are protected against infestation and rodent damage. Moreover, simple control records and periodic quantity verification are desirable procedures. Foods should be disbursed during specified hours and on various days to avoid a long wait by the recipient. Designated recipients can be assigned (or can select) preset pickup times to avoid congestion and delays that might deter their participation. Pickup presents an opportunity for nutrition education. Community members can easily handle most of these logistical tasks.

Product criteria and quantity

The products delivered should meet several criteria. They should have proven acceptability and be nutrient dense to avoid the bulkiness of staples that prevents small children from consuming adequate quantities. In addition, they should have at least a one-month shelf life, a requirement that may entail the use of preservatives or packaging in cans. Use of large reusable containers that the beneficiary could refill at the distribution point reduces the cost of packaging. This procedure might also reduce the risk of the product's resale. The form of the product and the container labeling should stress the intended user, as, for example, "baby food," or "for pregnant women only." Preparations should be graphically illustrated on the labels. Finally, the product should require little preparation and carry minimal risk of contamination or dilution; nutrition education should accompany the supplement distribution to reduce the risk of misuse. Economic behavior data should specify the circumstances of food preparation so that easily prepared foods are selected.

The final concern about the product is its quantity. The general cautions on availability and effect on price raised in the on-site feeding section also obtain here. The amount to be dispensed in each delivery can easily be calculated. The planners start with the nutrient deficit identified in the dietary survey. To the properly calculated dietary supplement they add an amount equal to the amount of the take-home portion that may be diverted to non-target persons. In this way, the target group's receipt of the nutrient increase is less problematic. In take-home programs in Colombia and the Dominican Republic, mothers fed the target children only about one-half of the ration and gave the remainder to other children.[5] Although take-home programs incur a sharing leakage unknown in on-site programs, the take-home program can reach about four times more target-group members than can the on-site program.[6]

A further leakage threatening the program's objective is the previously mentioned substitution effect, in which the supplement diminishes normal food expenditures. Substitution of 45 percent was estimated in a Dominican Republic take-home program, but none occurred in surveyed Colombian and Pakistani programs.[7] It is doubtful that increased rations would reduce the substitution effect, which is caused by the family's income elasticity for food relative to other expenditures. A reduction might be achieved, however, through nutrition education.

5. Anderson, CARE *Preschool Nutrition Project,* pp. 34–36.
6. Ibid., p. 13.
7. Ibid., pp. 40–41.

Nutrient-dense Foods

The effectiveness of feeding programs, particularly the take-home variety, depends to a great extent on the product they deliver. Because nutrient-dense foods suitable for weaning are often unavailable to the target group even in the marketplace, their production may fill a nutritional void in the subsidized and commercial food-delivery systems. These foods can overcome the bulk constraint, meet deficiencies, and reduce leakages to nontarget groups. The principal design considerations for this intervention fall into three categories: processing, procurement, and marketing.

Processing

If the required nutrient mix and density can be obtained only through significant biological transformation—cooking, extrusion, or dehydration—production technology will be relatively capital intensive. If the transformation requires only cutting, grinding, and assembly of ingredients, a more labor-intensive, lower-technology process is possible. The nature of the raw material and of the final product, particularly toxicity potential and nutrient stability, will largely determine the production process. The more capital intensive it is, the greater the production volume needed, and the higher the probable foreign-exchange burden of imported equipment, though process and equipment modifications can sometimes decrease a chosen technology's capital intensity.

Over forty industrially processed nutrient-dense foods have been produced in developing countries: for example, Incaparina in Guatemala, Superamine in Algeria, Faffa in Ethiopia, Bienesta-rina in Colombia, Bal-Ahar in India, and Fortesan in Chile.[8] Several products have also been produced with simple technology in small, village-level processing operations. For example, in 1977 Nutripak in the Philippines was produced in eighty-seven small, municipal processing plants using simple grinding and packaging technology. Similarly, Hyderabad Mix was being provided to about 7,000 children in villages in the Hyderabad District of India. An even simpler technology for creating nutrient-dense foods consists of educating mothers to make "multimixes" by combining econom-

8. Elizabeth Orr, "The Contribution of New Food Mixtures to the Relief of Malnutrition, A Second Look," *Food and Nutrition,* vol. 3, no. 2 (1977), pp. 2–10.

ically available protein, calorie, and micronutrient sources into nutrient-rich and concentrated weaning foods. This approach relies fundamentally on nutrition education. Industrial processing may be more appropriate for urban areas in which large production levels are needed to realize economies of scale. The simple, small-scale technology and the multimix approaches have been used primarily in rural areas, but they might be feasible in servicing concentrated low-income urban communities. These approaches could create needed jobs in these communities and more effectively elicit community participation.

Nutritionists and food technologists should be consulted about the nature of food products and their manner of production. The local food-technology or nutrition institute could be the source of this expertise. Operating personnel can be hired, or existing government and private processing plants might be induced to manufacture this new product.

Procurement

The feasibility of the processing operation, like any agro-industrial project, hinges on its system of procuring raw materials. The system should be able to provide an adequate quantity of raw material of acceptable and stable quality at the right time for a reasonable price.[9] The new demand brought on by the procurement operation might raise prices unless concomitant efforts to increase supply are undertaken. It is particularly desirable to seek out nutritionally rich but underused crops that can provide additional nutrients without exacerbating the supply.[10] It may be necessary to use imported raw materials, but this alternative carries a foreign-exchange burden and exposes the program to the price variations and supply shortages endemic to international commodity markets. Dependence and supply uncertainties also crop up when donated food aid provides the raw material source, although such

9. James E. Austin, "A Systems Approach to Agro-industry Project Analysis," in *International Seminar in Tropical Agriculture and Livestock* (Mexico City: Fondo de Garantia, Banco de México, 1975), pp. 137–69; and *Agroindustrial Project Analysis* (Baltimore: Johns Hopkins University Press, forthcoming).

10. See, for example, Nevin Scrimshaw and others, *High Protein Product Development in Thailand*, Technical Report no. 1 (Cambridge, Mass.: Massachusetts Institute of Technology, MIT International Nutrition Planning Program, 1973).

food aid might be used during the initial phase of production of weaning food until the local supply becomes adequate.

Marketing

The marketing aspect of the operation involves product testing, market segmentation, distribution, packaging, promotion, and pricing. As part of the product development effort, new foods should be tested for organoleptic acceptability, cultural compatibility, and ease of preparation. This research should involve studies of consumer food practices and beliefs, as well as in-home product testing.

Alternative market outlets for new formulated foods are institutional programs and commercial stores. Though targeted nutrition programming is usually concerned only with the former, both should be considered, since if both are serviced, greater volume and economies of scale might be possible. Having the product on the market and perhaps even marketing it to middle-income families might prevent its acquiring a "poor-man's food" image, and thereby enhance its acceptability to lower-income consumers. The existence of a guaranteed government market might also increase food processors' incentive to invest in the product. By having the food simultaneously on the market and in feeding programs, the probability is increased that its use will be continued after the feeding program is discontinued or after individual families end their participation in it (assuming a sufficiently low price).

Data on the location of commercial retail outlets and the target group's shopping patterns will help determine the best channels for distributing food to the target group. Employing wholesalers might be helpful, but their markups should be scrutinized for their effect on retail prices and on the ability of the target group to pay. Although food can be distributed directly to retailers to achieve more precise targeting, this requires a fleet of delivery vehicles and a sales force.

Packaging will depend greatly on the market outlet selected. If commercial channels are used, packaging should prevent insect penetration and provide a three- to six-month shelf life. Such packaging can, unfortunately, be expensive and often obtainable only by import. Institutional feeding, as mentioned earlier, has the advantage of requiring only bulk packaging or less expensive materials for unit packaging.

Any new product requires promotion for successful marketing through commercial channels. To popularize nutritious foods, commercial promotion might be effective in a broad strategy of nutrition education, especially in conjunction with an institutional feeding program. The government can assist the promotional effort by giving its seal of approval or by providing free broadcasting or other promotional facilities.

The final marketing element to be considered is pricing, which has been a major barrier to commercial attempts in marketing high nutrition foods.[11] Subsidizing the marketing operation may be necessary to reach the most disadvantaged groups. This subsidy can be paid directly or indirectly to the processor in tax relief or by exemption from duty. Alternatively, the processor can offer a higher-priced version of the product to upper-income consumers and subsidize a cheaper product for the poor with the profits from that line. In some instances the government may wish to manufacture the product itself, but even where this capability exists, using the private sector and perhaps subsidizing some of the costs may be the most cost-effective and socially advantageous approach.

Ration Shops

Government-operated stores distributing staples at subsidized prices exist in urban areas in many countries; they are directed primarily at overcoming the income constraint on healthy diets. Since urban dwellers are almost totally dependent on the market system, they are particularly exposed to the nutritional risk accompanying commodity price rises, but they are also more politically vocal in opposing such increases. Three aspects of ration shops as a form of intervention require analysis: level of subsidy, selection of commodities, and selection of participants.

Level of subsidy

The level of subsidy will partly reflect the income of the target group, its price elasticity of demand for the ration product, and its

11. Elizabeth Orr, *The Use of Protein-Rich Foods for the Relief of Malnutrition in Developing Countries: An Analysis of Experience* (London: Tropical Products Institute, 1972).

cross-elasticity of demand for other products. Elasticity estimates are not always available, but they can sometimes be derived from household-expenditure surveys and time series of consumer prices.[12] Low-income urban consumers generally have a high price elasticity because a large portion of their expenditure goes for food.[13] In view of this elasticity, the subsidy must be cleverly devised so that incremental consumption will eradicate the nutritional deficit. Diversion of expenditure to nonfood items or substitution for less nutritional food can be high, depending on the elasticities.

The most serious consideration in setting the subsidy level is the burden imposed on the government's budget. Procurement price less resale price and administrative costs constitutes the amount of the subsidy. If agricultural prices rise, the subsidy level can become inordinately large unless the government can raise the resale price. Subsidies should be adjusted to inflation rates to ensure that the beneficiaries' real purchasing power is preserved.

A further concern is to prevent subsidized retail prices from lowering farm prices and depressing food production. Price supports can help avoid this disincentive effect. Added demand for farm products might result, however, in a short-run increase in commodity prices, depending on supply elasticities. Clearly, planning that coordinates supply and demand is indispensable. Availability of supply through domestic production and imports and corresponding response rates should be estimated as an integral part of program management.

Selection of commodities

The planner selects the quantity of the ration and the type of the commodity. Quantity must be limited to restrict the subsidy costs and avoid disruption of the supply market. The quantity should be sufficient, of course, to make a significant contribution to the solution of the nutritional problem. To achieve this goal the family ra-

12. For example, see Philip Musgrove, *Consumer Behavior in Latin America: Income and Spending in Ten Andean Cities* (Washington, D.C.: Brookings Institution, 1978), pp. 195–203.

13. For example, see Desmond McCarthy, "Nutrition, Food, and Prices in Pakistan," Discussion Paper no. 4 (Cambridge, Mass.: Massachusetts Institute of Technology, MIT International Nutrition Planning Program, 1975).

tion must usually be more generous than the identified nutritional deficit to compensate for leakages such as storage loss and resale.

If the chosen commodity requires only minimal dietary change, the program will probably be accepted by the target group. The product's quality can even be enhanced by fortification. New nutrient-dense foods call for considerable promotion and nutrition education if they are to be used as the subsidized product. The use of new foods or of commodities consumed particularly by low-income families tends to decrease, respectively, leakage to nontarget-group family members and resale to healthy families.[14]

Participation

Ration shops may be either open or selective. The open shop has the advantage of reducing administrative work in applying a nutritional or economic-means test, but it increases the risk that well-off families will consume funds needed for nutritionally impoverished families. The selective approach reduces overcoverage but increases the administrative burden. Both systems are used. For example, Pakistan's ration shops use the open approach, and Mexico's subsidized milk dispensaries employ a selective process involving individual family interviews and computer-dispensed ration cards with dispensing times precoded as to day and hour. Administrative capacities vary, so varying levels of sophistication are feasible.

The risk of overcoverage in an open system can be reduced by the use of a specialized commodity, as mentioned above, or by locating the shop in low-income areas. In the closed system, ration cards or similar means of identification are needed after eligibility has been established. Special packaging can reduce resale under either system.

The accessibility to targeted beneficiaries of ration shops and the certain availability of the product are also critical to participation. This requires that the government give special attention to allocating the requisite managerial, organizational, and logistical resources to the system.

---

14. Beatrice Lorge Rogers and F. James Levinson discuss the "self-selection" targeting phenomenon that occurs through the use of a "poor-man's food" in Pakistani ration shops in "Subsidized Food Consumption Systems in Low-Income Countries: The Pakistan Experience," Discussion Paper no. 6 (Cambridge, Mass.: Massachusetts Institute of Technology, MIT International Nutrition Planning Program, April 1976).

Food-coupon Programs

A food-coupon program is similar to the ration-shop intervention except that it uses a private rather than a public food-distribution system. The previous discussion of subsidy level, commodity type, and participation generally apply to a food-coupon system, but its administrative pecularities merit special consideration.

A food-coupon system has four basic steps: certification of the participant, issuance of the coupons, coupon conversion to food, and coupon reimbursement.

Certification

Several criteria for eligibility are possible. In the United States, for example, the Food Stamp Program uses income criteria, whereas the more precisely targeted Women, Infants, and Children Program employs primarily the criterion of nutritional risk. The former is basically a program to supplement family income; the latter is directed at specific family members and tied to particular foods. Both use coupons. To reduce administrative procedures and cost, entire zones of a city might be considered eligible for the program. Within these areas, all pregnant or lactating women or mothers of preschoolers could be deemed eligible. Such eligibility is currently being applied in Colombia. Other indirect, nutritional-risk factors mentioned in the nutritional-status indicators section of this paper could also be applied. More stringent nutritional criteria such as second- and third-degree malnutrition could be used, although they require anthropometric measurements.

Issuance

The allocation of coupons involves the designer in questions of form, quantity, frequency, and location. The three design criteria are administrative simplicity, maximum security, and minimum cost. The coupon itself should be difficult to forge, perhaps bound in booklets, signed upon issuance, and countersigned upon conversion. Coupons printed by the treasury are a possibility, but they are probably too costly.

The number of coupons given to a family will depend on the number of its members in the target group and a predetermined relation between the average dietary gap and the amount of food needed to fill it. It is recommended that the coupons be restricted to specific foods. The simplest approach is to make one coupon good for one package of a specified food.

With this arrangement, the number of coupons distributed at any one time will depend on the frequency of disbursement. A two-week supply of coupons reduces the frequency, inconvenience, and cost of coupon disbursement, and at the same time it does not allow the beneficiary an excess of coupons and food, which could tempt resale. When food is purchased daily, as is common in urban areas, a two-week disbursement seems reasonable. Thus, for example, if each package contained enough nutrients to fill the weekly deficit of a preschooler (with an additional amount to compensate for estimated intrafamilial and other leakages), two coupons for each preschooler can be dispensed biweekly. Similar arrangements can be made for other target beneficiaries.

Maximum participation rests, in large measure, on the location of coupon-disbursement centers, which should be accessible and open at convenient hours. Clinics, schools, post offices, and day-care and community-development centers can serve as coupon dispensaries. If certifiers act as dispensers, personnel economies will result. Furthermore, coupon distribution might be used to attract people to health centers or nutrition-education classes.

Conversion

Conversion refers to the issue of who will accept the coupons, for what products, and how.

A strength of the coupon system derives from its use of an existing network of stores rather than a new government network of ration shops or subsidized stores that incur infrastructure costs and can cause management problems. Indirect measures are needed, however, to exercise control over the private system. Participating stores should be selected for proximity and patronage by target-group families. Store managers should be fully informed of the coupon system and agree to dispense the designated foods in stock only for coupons. The incentive to participate is the guaranteed demand for the products, a set margin of profit for the store's service, and the attraction of customers to the store.

The products should be specified to the target group as, for example, weaning foods or special foods appropriate to pregnant and lactating mothers. Issuing coupons valid for these foods alone targets the program more precisely and reduces leakage, which is possible on a large scale, particularly in a general food-stamp program in which the product is a common staple. In the initial stages a highly desirable product—for example, sugar or oil—might be included along with the special weaning food to enhance the system's popularity. An adequate supply of the product must be assured prior to implementation, and increases must be coordinated with larger issues of coupons.

One coupon is exchanged for a unit of food, but, in addition to the coupon, the beneficiaries might pay some sum to reduce program costs. This policy will encourage a habit of purchasing the product that might continue after the subsidy is reduced or eliminated. Furthermore, payment might erase a possible welfare stigma associated with the program. .

Reimbursement

Store owners are unlikely to participate unless they are reimbursed for the coupons simply, quickly, and dependably. Two major reimbursement alternatives exist. Store owners can redeem the coupons at banks for cash and a margin, and the banks can pass on the coupons to the national treasury or central bank for credit. Alternatively, store owners can give the coupons plus the margin to wholesalers in payment for more program merchandise. This alternative assumes that the retailers will have been paid their margin by the coupon carriers. The wholesaler does the same with the food processor and the government reimburses the processor. This arrangement limits governmental administration to interaction with a few industrialists rather than with a multitude of retailers; it also reduces the possibility of retailers' exchanging coupons for cash or for foods other than those designated.

Fortification

Fortification attempts to improve the quality of a population's diet by adding nutrients to foods it already eats. It is particularly relevant where the foods in the diet do not adequately provide specific nutrients. Such diet deficiencies are usually the result of low income, food beliefs, processing practices, or health and environmental factors.

Four main aspects of this intervention should be considered: nutritional need, structure of the commodity system, fortification technology, and consumer acceptance.[15]

Nutritional need

Protein deficiencies can be remedied by fortification of foods with synthetic amino acids or protein supplements. The laws of nutritional metabolism, however, make protein fortification wasteful unless caloric deficits are also remedied. Dietary surveys show a greater incidence of calorie than of protein deficiency, although the latter is sometimes understated because amino-acid balance and biological value are not always considered. Where the dietary staple, though satisfactory in calories, is particularly deficient in protein—as is cassava—macrofortification merits consideration as part of an intervention mix. One of the advantages of fortification is that the increase in protein occurs without increasing the physical quantity of grain consumed, thereby reducing the bulk constraint facing preschoolers consuming staples. Another advantage is that fortification places no additional price pressure on agricultural supply.

Micronutrient deficiencies such as vitamin A and iron anemias are even more prevalent than the macroshortages, and fortification is particularly appropriate for alleviating them. The dramatic reduction of goiter by the iodization of salt illustrates the potentiality of micronutrient fortification.

Micro- and macrofortification may have to be considered together in some instances. For example, vitamin A deficiency may arise because of the failure of the liver to synthesize sufficient retinol-binding protein for lack of protein calories, suggesting that simultaneous protein supplementation and vitamin A fortification might be advisable.[16] The starting task, as suggested previously, is to identify clearly which deficiencies exist, assess their severity, and locate those who are afflicted.

15. For a more detailed discussion of these factors, see James E. Austin (ed.), *Global Malnutrition and Cereal Grain Fortification* (Cambridge, Mass.: Ballinger Publishing Co., 1979).

16. David I. Thurnham, "Through Science and Nutrition to Human Well-Being," *Food Policy*, vol. 1, no. 1 (November 1975), pp. 74–76.

Structure of the commodity system

Once the need is identified, a determination must be made on how to reach the target group. This decision requires an examination of various carriers, such as wheat flour, sugar, salt, and the like. The chosen carrier must be consumed regularly by the target group, and must in the commodity system pass through a processing point where fortification can take place. The dietary habits, food-purchasing patterns, and movements of the target group should be examined to see if these requirements exist.

Conventional wisdom has held that centralized carrier processing is prerequisite to fortification.[17] The rationale for this assertion is that the fewer the processing points, the easier and more economical the control and management of the intervention. If only a few mills supply most of the population, however, there will be overcoverage, since nutrients will also be provided to those who do not need them. Decentralized milling of cereals in rural areas permits more accurate targeting.[18] Although urban areas are more likely to have centralized milling, some products (for example, broken rice or bulgur) may be consumed principally by lower-income groups.[19] These products can be fortified at the central mill. Targeting by staple will always entail some overcoverage because within the family all members consume the product, not just preschoolers and pregnant and lactating women.

17. For example, the Protein Advisory Group (PAG) stated that "the processing of the carrier food should be relatively centralized," in FAO/WHO/UNICEF Protein Advisory Group, "PAG Statement on Amino-Acid Fortification of Foods," Statement no. 9 (New York: United Nations, August 24, 1970), p. 12. The Joint FAO/WHO/Expert Committee on Nutrition similarly asserted in its *Eighth Report*: "it is desirable that a single centre be designated within the region or country."

18. Almost all rural families, even subsistence farmers, appear to use commercial mills to grind their grain rather than do it themselves, thus permitting fortification at the village level. This would be desirable where the nutrient deficiency was concentrated in a certain region rather than across the whole country. See James E. Austin and Donald Snodgrass, "Cereal Fortification: Barriers to Implementation," *Improving the Nutrient Quality of Cereals II* (Washington, D.C.: Agency for International Development [AID], September 1976), pp. 241–54.

19. A similar example of "atta" wheat in India is discussed by F. James Levinson and David Call in "Nutrition Intervention in Low-Income Countries: A Planning Model and Case Study," Cornell International Agricultural Development Mimeograph no. 34 (Ithaca: Cornell University, 1970), pp. 23–27.

Technology

After locating a vehicle that will reach the target group and that has an accessible processing point, an assessment must be made of the technological feasibility of finding a fortificant and a fortifying process appropriate to the carrier.

Protein fortificants—synthetic amino acids or natural protein supplements—and vitamin and mineral premixes are all produced commercially and present no major technical problems. The difficulties, to the extent that they exist, relate more to combining the fortificant properly with the vehicle and to processing and cooking. These problems have solutions, as shown by the successful fortification of bread with protein, sugar with vitamin A, and salt with iodine. Absorption difficulties had been encountered with iron fortification of salt, but in India ferric orthophosphate has recently been combined successfully with sodium bisulphate to promote adsorption in fortified salt.

In assessing the technical feasibility of a fortificant, the course of the product through consumption should be followed in order to spot possible losses in nutritional integrity in storage (decomposition or settling), cooking (heat damage or liquid discard), and absorption. A trace nutrient such as riboflavin permits easy verification of intake.

A final aspect of the fortifying process is the reaction of food processors to the intervention. If their cooperation is not forthcoming, the intervention is doomed. Consequently, the probable operational and economic effects of fortification on their operations should be carefully assessed to determine the necessary incentives to ensure their collaboration.[20] Making fortification legally mandatory might work, but if incremental costs are high, processors may circumvent the law or pass on the costs in higher prices to the consumer. This resistance could affect the next variable.

Consumer acceptance

A commonly cited advantage of fortification is that consumers accept it because it does not affect the carrier's appearance or organoleptic characteristics. But invisibility should not be taken for

20. Micronutrient fortification is less expensive than macrofortification, so it would be less objectionable to processors.

granted, since consumers have been able to discern the alteration, especially with iron or protein fortification.[21] Formal, blind taste tests should be employed before launching a program. If differences are discernible, it should be determined whether they make the product more or less appetizing.

Invisibility is impossible if the beneficiaries bring their own grain to mills for grinding and fortification. Visibility might, however, be desirable where parents must give the product to certain family members and where they have to pay more for it, because without visibility the reason for the price premium would not be evident.

Direct Nutrient Dosage

This intervention involves programs that deliver nutrients directly in concentrated form. Instead of being added to another food, as in fortification, the nutrient is given separately and directly to the target group. The most common forms of this intervention have been massive distributions of vitamin A and iron pills. The two basic design issues for the intervention concern nutrient form and the delivery system.

Nutrient form

Depending on their characteristics, nutrients can be dispensed in the form of pills, liquids, or injections. Oral pills are particularly convenient in that they are highly storable, transportable, and acceptable. The pill is the technologically appropriate form for most minerals and vitamins; multinutrient pills are also feasible. The size of the pill—the dosage—depends on the magnitude of the deficiency, absorptive capacity, and the delivery system.

Delivery system

Vitamin A deficiencies, more than others, have been addressed by direct-dosage programs. Because the vitamin is storable in the body, infrequent massive doses (two to four times a year) are all

21. See, for example, Charles Puttkamer, "Fortification of Salt with Iron—India," *Workshop on Food Fortification*, AID (Washington, D.C.: AID, May 1972), pp. 41–45. See also Austin (ed.), *Global Malnutrition*, chap. 5.

that is needed. Sometimes an infrastructure exists, such as malaria monitors or immunization teams, that can distribute the dosage. A problem with direct-dosage programs not shared by fortification is that each administration requires a separate delivery effort. It is not a continuous process and therefore each time faces organizational and budgetary obstacles. Another difficulty is the greater effort required of the beneficiaries to come to a center to get the dose, and to remember to take it—burdens that can cause significant participatory declines over time, as was the case in a vitamin A program in Bangladesh.[22]

Food Processing and Distribution

Structural and human inefficiencies and exploitation in the existing food system raise food prices and lead to nutritionally adverse consumption patterns. Consequently, improvements in the food system through infrastructural, organizational, and regulatory interventions are desirable.

Infrastructure

Inadequacy of roads to interior rural areas, of storage facilities, and of transport equipment can cause significant postharvest food loss. This loss is seldom documented, but has been estimated at about 30 percent. A loss of this magnitude obviously increases prices in the cities.

Public marketplaces constitute a second infrastructural weakness common to urban centers. Often these places are old, unhygienic, overcrowded, and inefficient, and, with the city's expansion, they are enveloped and their originally favorable locations become unsuitable. New wholesale markets and strategically located satellite markets can trim inefficiency in intermediate handling stages.[23] Improved storage facilities in the markets can reduce losses and

22. T. Stephen Jones, "The Mass Administration of Vitamin A: How Effective a Remedy of Xerophthalmia?," course paper (Cambridge, Mass.: Harvard School of Public Health, May 26, 1977).

23. Interviews in Mexico City verified that some produce passed through nine intermediaries before reaching the final consumer. See James E. Austin, "CONA-SUPO [Compania Nacional de Subsistencias Populares] and Rural Development: Program Description, Analysis and Recommendations" (a report submitted to the World Bank, December 1976), a restricted-circulation document, p. 48.

preserve nutritional quality, but such investments are often capital intensive, can reduce employment, and may disrupt social networks. Consequently, planned improvements should be preceded by a thorough analysis of the commodity system to document flows, margins, losses, and behavior. A new market structure will produce undesirable results unless it is accompanied by appropriate organizational changes.

Organization

Producers tend to be unorganized, leaving to multiple intermediaries the necessary assembly and transport functions. Their lack of organization leads to unnecessarily low farm prices and high handling costs. Farm marketing organizations are a possible source of achieving economies of scale in handling and transport and in improving terms of trade for the farmer. Well-organized farmers may be able to expand into the processing and wholesaling stages of the industry.

The marketing system's operation will be further improved by creating a price information system to help farmers and consumers make more informed selling and buying decisions. Daily broadcasts of prevailing prices in the wholesale markets can work well, given a broad ownership of transistor radios.

Retailer associations or consumer cooperatives can make purchases as a group to counterbalance the power of large wholesalers, achieving economies from quantity purchases and shared transport costs. Food processors can also join together to share expenses for market research and for development of techniques to enhance nutrition.

Regulation

Government regulation may be called for in several areas. Hygiene and sanitation standards for food processors should be established and enforced through an inspection system. Guidelines for the use of food ingredients should also be set and products labeled as to their content.

Food-processing technology should also be monitored for its effect on nutritional quality. Deleterious technology such as rice polishing should be discouraged and nutritionally enhancing processes such as parboiling encouraged by import restrictions, tax credits, or other regulatory mechanisms.

Food processors' promotional activities should also be watched. Among other causes of undesirable trends, advertising that might lead to adverse nutritional behavior—for example, increased infant-formula usage and decreased breastfeeding—should be reviewed. Processors should be encouraged to join in efforts to promote improved nutritional habits and products.

A final form of regulation is economic, through price controls or subsidies. Price controls are frequently instituted to preclude price speculation or exploitation in consumer staples, but enforcement of these controls is often difficult to administer. General price subsidies are costly, however, because they also subsidize even the well-to-do.[24] Furthermore, subsidies run the risk of discouraging farm production. As a more direct method of price regulation, the government can operate its own stores in low-income areas and compete with private outlets. The government's prices will tend to hold down prices generally. Alternatively, the government can enter the market at the wholesale level, buying and selling to influence prices.

Integrated Interventions

The various nutrition interventions considered above, far from being mutually exclusive, are complementary, and the planner should search for promising combinations. For example, nutrition education can often be effectively used in conjunction with feeding programs. Food production and distribution (that is, supply) interventions should be coordinated with programs, such as food coupons or on-site feeding, which increase demand.

In addition to combining direct programs, it is desirable to integrate nutrition interventions with other indirect programs, especially in health, water and sanitation, and family planning.

Rationale for integration

The first justification for integrating direct and indirect nutrition programs stems from the relation among factors contributing to

24. Shlomo Reutlinger and Marcelo Selowsky, *Malnutrition and Poverty: Magnitude and Policy Options*, World Bank Staff Occasional Papers, no. 23 (Baltimore: Johns Hopkins University Press, 1976), p. 5.

nutrition, health, and fertility. A review of the causes of mortality in several developing countries illustrates the dominant role of malnutrition, diarrheal disease, and pneumonia, which account for 36 percent to 65 percent of deaths among preschoolers (see Table 4-2). A review of integrated health and nutrition programs in the same countries also suggests that significant reduction in mortality is possible (see Table 4-3).

The synergy between infection and malnutrition has been well documented. Infectious diseases raise nutrient requirements and so increase vulnerability to malnutrition. The body's calorie expenditure even at rest rises as a result of the fever associated with infectious disease. Although this increased expenditure may indeed be less than the energy savings from reduced activity during illness, better data are needed on the activity level of the ill of various age groups to determine the net effect on calorie requirements. Nevertheless, disease decreases the efficiency of nutrient use even if the total requirement is lowered, and available food resources are consequently wasted.

Infectious disease can also increase the loss of essential nutrients as a result of subclinical malabsorption, diarrhea, or intestinal helminths. These symptoms can lead to catabolic nutrient losses or functional nutrient wastage deriving from nutrient overuse, sequestration, and diversion.

Food intake often falls during illness because of anorexia or cultural practice. In many cultures the quality and quantity of food fed to sick young children is reduced. A thin gruel often replaces the usual diet.

Birth trauma, infections such as neonatal tetanus and septicemia, and low birth weight may induce malnutrition by reducing the infant's ability to suckle. Conversely, malnutrition may lower the child's resistance to infection by the reduction of antibody synthesis in the presence of protein deficiency, the alteration of the cell-immune response associated with protein deficiency, and interference with tissue integrity. Less well-demonstrated but possible interactions include alterations in the gastrointestinal flora, changes in nonspecific resistance agents such as lysozomes, effects on nonspecific resistance to bacterial toxins, and changes in endocrine balance that alter defense mechanisms.

Furthermore, certain infections in pregnant women may harm the fetus even in the absence of fetal infection. Severe maternal infection can result in fetal death or premature labor, while less severe maternal infections seem to be involved in the pathogenesis

Table 4-2. *Cause of Death in Children under 5*
(percentage of total)

	Region			
Cause	Imesi, Nigeria, 1957	Narangwal, India, 1971–73[a]	Companiganj, Bangladesh, 1975[b]	Guatemala, 1956–57
Diarrheal disease	12	39	27	18
Pneumonia	12	19	7	19
Malnutrition	12	5	31	20
Malaria	8	0	0	0
Diphtheria, whooping cough, and tetanus	8	2	4	7
Smallpox	5	0	0	0
Measles	8	1	2	?
Tuberculosis	5	0	1	?
Anemia	0	0	0	?
Other, including neonatal deaths	30	34	28	37

Source: Colin McCord, "Medical Technology in Developing Countries: Useful, Useless, or Harmful?" (position paper for National Academy of Sciences Symposium on Effective Interventions to Reduce Infection in Malnourished Populations, Port-au-Prince, Haiti, June 12–16, 1977) (Washington, D.C.: National Academy of Sciences, Food and Nutrition Board, 1977); reprinted in *American Journal of Clinical Nutrition*, vol. 31 (November-December 1978), p. 2308. Used by permission of author and *Am. J. Clin. Nutr.*/American Society for Clinical Nutrition.
a. Children age 8 days to 3 years.
b. 1975 was a famine year.

of growth retardation. Concepts of the role of maternal infection and malnutrition in the pathogenesis of abnormal fetal growth are based on the correlation between maternal abnormality and the birth of infants small for their gestational age.

Combining nutrition programs with health measures appears promising. Immunization is also desirable. Although immunizable diseases account for only about 10 percent of preschool deaths in developing countries, they may precipitate malnutrition in many more children.[25] The interaction of malnutrition and infectious

25. Colin McCord, "Medical Technology in Developing Countries: Useful, Useless, or Harmful?" (position paper for National Academy of Sciences Symposium on Effective Interventions to Reduce Infection in Malnourished Populations, Port-au-Prince, Haiti, June 12–16, 1977) (Washington, D.C.: National Academy of Sciences, Food and Nutrition Board, 1977); reprinted in *American Journal of Clinical Nutrition*, vol. 31 (November-December 1978), pp. 2301–13.

Table 4-3. *Mortality Rates in Four Integrated Mother-Child Health-Nutrition Programs*
(per 1,000 live births)

Region	Infant mortality rate			Mortality rate, ages 1–4		
	With inte-grated services	Without services[a]	Rate differ-ence (percent)	With inte-grated services	Without services	Rate differ-ence (percent)
Imesi, Nigeria	57.3	91.4[b]	−37.0	18.0	51.2	−64.8
Guatemala	55.4	84.7	−34.6	5.9	22.0[b]	−73.2
Narangwal, India	95.9	126.5	−24.2	10.1[c]	16.3[c]	−38.2
Jamkhed, India	39	97	−59.8	—	—	—

Source: Same as Table 4-2.
a. Population in service area.
b. From official statistics, which are probably low estimates.
c. Age 1 to 3 mortality rate.

disease also argues for the integration of nutrition with water and sanitation interventions.

The relation between water and health can be seen through White and Bradley's useful conceptual scheme.[26] Waterborne diseases are contracted from contaminated water; water-washed diseases stem from poor hygienic practices; water-based diseases depend on aquatic organisms for completion of their life cycles; and water-related insect vectors bite or breed near water. Specific water-related diseases are contracted as follows:

Waterborne diseases	Water-washed diseases	Water-based diseases	Water-vectored diseases
Cholera	Shigellosis	Schistosomiasis	Malaria
Infectious hepatitis	Scabies	Guinea worm	Sleeping sickness
Typhoid	Trachoma		Yellow fever

Water interventions can be characterized as focused on quantity or quality, depending on the disease-water relations. For example, general diarrheas, which are usually transmitted by personal con-

26. G. F. White, D. J. Bradley, and A. U. White, *Drawers of Water* (Chicago: University of Chicago Press, 1972).

tact, are classified as water-washed diseases; they are more amenable to eradication by water quantity than quality.[27] For waterborne, -based, or -vectored diseases, water quality appears more critical.

In densely populated urban areas, the risk of epidemics from waterborne and water-washed diseases is particularly high. Because contamination from interruption in the central service system or from industrial pollution is possible, water quality is especially important.[28]

When water interventions are instituted, environmental sanitation must be considered as well as the behavioral patterns of water usage. Pure piped water does little good if home-cooking practices are unsanitary or storage facilities are contaminated. Investing in physical facilities alone may therefore prove insufficient. Although water interventions appear desirable, understanding of the complex relations among nutrition, infection, and water remains inadequate and is obscured by differences among ecological systems.

The relation between population control and nutrition has given rise to several hypotheses. One suggests female malnutrition raises the age of menarche and lowers that of menopause, reducing fecundity. Since it seems desirable to avert increases in population that could accompany better maternal nutrition, projects should be coordinated both to improve maternal nutrition and to increase the accessibility of fertility control.

A second, "child-survival" hypothesis proposes that a reduction in infant and child mortality lowers fertility rates by reducing the number of births necessary to guarantee a desirable family size.[29]

27. John Briscoe, "The Role of Water Supply in Improving Health in Poor Countries" (position paper for the National Academy of Sciences Symposium on Effective Interventions to Reduce Infection in Malnourished Populations, Port-au-Prince, Haiti, June 12–16, 1977) (Washington, D.C.: National Academy of Sciences, Food and Nutrition Board, 1977); reprinted in *American Journal of Clinical Nutrition*, vol. 31 (November-December 1978), pp. 2100–13.

28. Robert E. Schneider, M. Shiffman, and Jacques Faigenblum, "The Potential Effect of Water on Gastrointestinal Infections Prevalent in Developing Countries (with Special Reference to Bangladesh)" (position paper for the National Academy of Sciences Symposium on Effective Interventions to Reduce Infection in Malnourished Populations, Port-au-Prince, Haiti, June 12–16, 1977) (Washington, D.C.: National Academy of Sciences, Food and Nutrition Board, 1977); reprinted in *American Journal of Clinical Nutrition*, vol. 31 (November-December 1978), pp. 2089–99.

29. Joe Wray, "Will Better Nutrition Decrease Fertility?" *Proceedings of the 9th Congress on Nutrition, Mexico 1972* (Basel: Karger, 1975), pp. 16–31.

The underlying mechanism is poorly understood. Couples aware of the greater likelihood of child survival may choose to have fewer births, or the economic pressures of increased survival may reduce births. Although data on the "demographic transition" show that birthrates decline as infant and child mortality rates fall, many socioeconomic changes complicate the search for causes. Yet evidence that fertility declines with the reduction of infant and child mortality suggests that health services and an environmental sanitation project could enhance the acceptance of family planning. Services that increase the mother's ability to lactate and the infant's desire and ability to suckle can also be conceived of as family planning services because of the contraceptive effect of lactation.

The reverse interaction of fertility on infant, child, and maternal health and nutritional status has also been proposed. The high correlation between birth order or low birth weight and child mortality has been discussed.[30] The nutritional deprivation of the child following poorly spaced pregnancies has also been described in discussions of the high incidence of malnutrition in the second year of life, when the pregnant mother no longer breastfeeds her child. Because high fertility rates and poor child spacing are costly to the nutritional health of mothers and children, family-planning measures can significantly improve health and nutrition.

In addition to the effect of nutrition, health, and family planning programs, there are potential operational benefits from integration. The major economic benefits derive from economies of combination, since joint use of facilities capitalizes on fixed-cost investments. A common delivery system can also economize on beneficiaries' time and reduce inconvenience by offering multiple services during a single visit. It may also economize on scarce management resources. Where the target groups of different interventions are identical or are located in the same area, such economies are feasible and, of course, desirable.

Operational effects can also be enhanced by integration because the delivery system becomes more flexible. Furthermore, the provision of one service can increase credibility and improve receptivity to other services.[31]

30. Ruth Puffer and Carlos Serrano, *Patterns of Mortality in Childhood* (Washington, D.C.: Pan American Health Organization, 1975).

31. James E. Austin and F. James Levinson, "Population and Nutrition: A Case for Integration," *Milbank Memorial Fund Quarterly, Health and Society* (Spring 1974), pp. 169–84.

Integration points

Though it can adopt many forms and be pursued with varying degrees of intensity, integration should always be adapted to the situation it addresses. There is no standard formula, but the most promising activities for integration appear to be community diagnosis; target group identification; community surveillance; procurement, delivery, and storage of supplies; provision of services; promotion of programs; development of educational materials; training and supervision; and data analysis and evaluation.

The extent of integration depends on the existence of shareable infrastructures, personnel, data, and target groups. A possible result of intensive combined activities is increased program cost that may reach or exceed traditional nonintegrated budget ceilings, although the cost for unit of service or for beneficiary may decline. Thus, budget comparisons should consider the total of the two budgets that would have been necessary for the two individual interventions.

A further programming issue centers on whether to carry out the integration sequentially or simultaneously. Building on an intervention in progress has the advantage of reducing organizational complexity and managerial demands, but its drawback, in addition to the lack of initial synergy, is that the superimposition of a new program on an existing operation may be disruptive and difficult. Furthermore, the efficiencies possible in combined training will be lost. Which combinations and what order of sequence are most desirable is unclear from the existing data.

Disadvantages

Counterbalancing the potential benefits of integration, whether of direct or indirect nutrition programs or of different types of direct interventions, are possible disadvantages. The following should be recognized:

- Staff can be overloaded with work. This risk is especially high for the village-level worker, and can result in a dilution of all efforts or the neglect of some.
- One unpopular component can lower the acceptance of the entire package.
- Curative programs may dominate preventive ones because of their apparently greater urgency and more dramatic results.

- Control may be more difficult when more activities are integrated into a single project. Problems of cost and time allocations and of tradeoffs are likely to arise.
- When numerous objectives compete for staff attention, evaluation becomes more difficult.
- Although more efficient, support services may become more complicated. Deliveries of materials from different supply sources, arriving on different schedules, exemplify increased logistical complexities.
- The desire for integration efficiency may overshadow considerations of effectiveness.
- Workers from one sector may be inadequately trained in the substance of accompanying programs, and may therefore tend to neglect them.
- Managerial requirements can exceed available administrative capacity.
- Cooperating organizations can offer institutional resistance.

In spite of these drawbacks, the potential benefits of integration are sufficient to justify considerable effort in fitting programs together for maximum synergy. To summarize, interventions are not mutually exclusive, but can often be synergistically combined. Although empirical data on optimal combinations of intervention or desired sequencing are as yet unavailable, the analyst should attempt to design a portfolio of programs that will address in the broadest possible way the nutritional needs of the various identified target groups. Different mixes of interventions might be appropriate for different cities or for different groups within a single city. Moreover, urban nutrition interventions should be considered and planned in the context of a general urban and rural nutrition program. Finally, a nutrition intervention should not be thought of in isolation from other health, population, or economic interventions. An integrated approach is essential for avoiding inefficiency and for realizing the program's potential.

5

•–

Evaluation

The planner obviously faces the task of choosing among the intervention options considered in the previous chapter. Again, rather than being mutually exclusive, the alternatives are generally complementary. The objective of selection is to develop the best combination of interventions to address the multiple causes of malnutrition. Although some compromise has to be accepted, three general criteria are applicable.

First, it must be possible to implement the intervention. All interventions potentially confront a series of managerial, political, economic, and social barriers that can hinder implementation. The more serious and less superable the barriers, the less feasible the intervention. Second, the intervention must be repeatable. Too often small-scale pilot projects work well initially but fail when their scope is expanded. If the intervention cannot serve significant numbers continuously, it is not desirable. Third, it must be cost effective. The resources interventions consume must be examined relative to the nutritional benefits they provide. Interventions with the lowest cost-effectiveness ratios are the most desirable.

Note: The section "Costing methods" benefited from the methodological work of Donald Snodgrass and James Kocher of the Harvard Institute of International Development. The section "Analysis of Cost Effectiveness" is derived primarily from James E. Austin, "The Perilous Journey of Nutrition Evaluation" (position paper for the National Academy of Sciences Symposium on Effective Interventions to Reduce Infection in Malnourished Populations, Port-au-Prince, Haiti, June 12–16, 1977) (Washington, D.C.: National Academy of Sciences, Food and Nutrition Board, 1977); revised in the *American Journal of Clinical Nutrition,* vol. 31 (November-December 1978), pp. 2324–38. The estimative indicators contained in the section "Ratio indicators of cost-benefit" are based primarily on the comments and thoughtful work of David Dapice of Tufts University.

Often intervention selection will have to be made in the absence of empirical data on cost or effectiveness. In these instances outside experience and expected performance must be relied upon, and the intervention should be subjected to periodic review and revision. Accordingly, a program to monitor performance should be instituted concurrently with implementation so as to gather necessary data on cost effectiveness. The types of financial and costing analyses needed for evaluating performance require careful consideration.

The selection of the intervention encompasses analyses of finance and cost effectiveness, the subjects of this chapter; the potential barriers to implementation are considered in chapter 6.

Financial Analysis

In examining the financial aspects of an intervention, costing methods, leakage, and balance-of-payment and fiscal implications are particularly important.

Costing methods

Standard costing procedure should be followed to evaluate the intervention properly. All program costs should first be estimated. One type of costing is the market-price approach, which values project requirements at their accounting value (their actual cost to the project); a second is the social-cost approach, which attaches a value to any resource used in the project that has an alternative social value, whether or not the project paid cash for the resource.

Social costing is preferable for evaluation. To arrive at this cost it is necessary to list all project requirements, to attach their market prices, and to adjust these market prices to social cost, using, if necessary, shadow prices.[1]

---

1. For more detailed explanation of shadow pricing and cost-benefit analysis techniques, see Michael Roemer and Joseph Stern, *The Appraisal of Development Projects* (New York: Praeger Publishers, 1975), and Lyn Squire and Herman G. van der Tak, *Economic Analysis of Projects* (Baltimore: Johns Hopkins University Press, 1975).

Project accounting systems are often rudimentary and neglected by project directors who, lacking formal managerial training, do not understand or appreciate the importance of a costing system. Even where reasonably accurate cost records are kept, other problems deserve highlighting. First, project needs that do not incur a cash disbursement but do represent a social cost are often neither identified nor accounted for because they do not fit into the standard accounting system. A system to evaluate data should include a simple record of these needs, and a costing evaluation should attach a value to them.

Allocating shared costs constitutes a second problem. Nutrition programs often consist of multiple components involving the same personnel or shared facilities. Unless costs are allocated equitably, one component may bear a disproportionate share of the costs. No cost should be attributed to an activity if it would have been incurred anyway. That cost is not due to the project; only incremental costs are assignable. The principle of marginality is difficult to apply to integrated programs because it is not always clear what is marginal to what. An alternative is to allocate costs across the components on a basis such as time spent or space occupied by workers.

Leakage

Leakage is potentially the most costly aspect of interventions involving food distribution.

Leakages comprise all losses of the commodities delivered to the target population. These losses may derive from damage, infestation, pilferage, diversion to healthy families or nonvulnerable members of needy families, inability to consume adequate quantities of food because of bulk constraint, or inefficient nutrient use by the body due to illness or malabsorption. Most losses from leakage are not so serious as losses from spoilage or improper storage. In cost effectiveness, however, leakage has major implications, since, in order to get a certain quantity of nutrients to the target group, the program must deliver that amount plus a surplus to offset the leakage.

In determining a suitable intervention, both direct and control costs should be examined. The former is the total cost of a certain amount of nutrient delivered to the target population, including leakage. The latter comprises the administrative and managerial expenses involved in reducing unintended consumption and cutting direct costs. It is conceivable that elaborate means tests may inflate control costs over the direct costs they are intended to reduce.

Several types of leakage have been examined for the extent of loss they involve. Estimates are extremely difficult to make accurately, but it is clear that their economic importance is so great that considerable effort is warranted in gathering the necessary data. Empirical data on losses are scarce and imperfect, but the following list reveals the relative importance of each leakage. It should be noted that these are tentative estimates subject to further verification.[2]

Leakage	Percentage of loss
Before distribution to consumers	
Shipping and handling	5
Pilferage	5
On- and off-farm storage	2–10
After distribution to consumers	
Nontarget-group consumption	0–40
Reselling	≤30
Sharing within family	0–90
Substitution of regular food by aid food	≥0–60
Changed expenditure pattern	0–50
Bulk constraint	0–20
Malabsorption	4
Loss or spoilage in the home	5–10

The magnitude of these postdistribution losses points out the necessity of including leakage estimates in cost projections. Table 5-1 presents a matrix of the various interventions considered earlier and the leakage they are likely to experience. Design should be oriented partly toward reducing this leakage in the ways suggested.

Balance-of-payment and fiscal implications

In an assessment of interventions, leakage and other operating costs can, for purposes of comparison, be converted into measures such as cost per kilocalorie delivered to a target-group member.

2. Leakage estimates are from James E. Austin (ed.), *Urban Malnutrition: Problem Assessment and Intervention Guidelines* (Cambridge, Mass.: Harvard University, 1976), pp. 126–46. The work of John Dixon and Henry Nieder was particularly useful in making these estimates. The malabsorption leakage was calculated by John Briscoe.

Table 5-1. *Matrix of Leakage from Interventions*

	Leakage								
Intervention	*Shipping and handling*	*Storage*	*Pilferage*	*Resale*	*Intra-familial sharing*	*Bulk constraint*	*Malabsorption*	*Substitution for regular food*	*Nontarget-family coverage*
Nutrition education					X	X	X		X
On-site feeding									
Traditional staple	X	X	X			X	X	X	
Nutrition-dense food	X	X	X				X	X	
Take-home feeding									
Traditional staple	X	X	X	X	X	X	X	X	
Nutrient-dense food	X	X	X	X	X		X	X	
Ration shop[a]	X	X	X	X	X	X	X	X	X
Food coupon[b]				X	X		X	X	
Fortification					X	X	X		X
Direct nutrient dosage	X						X		
Food-processing distribution	X	X							

a. Assumes no means test.
b. Assumes a means test and nutrient-dense foods.

90

These unitary cost indexes should, however, be extrapolated to total costs for the entire target group to permit comparison with the available resources. In this regard, care must also be taken to project financial estimates beyond the start-up phase, since what might seem financially feasible on a pilot scale can become economically unrealistic as the program expands. If total cost exceeds available funds, either the number of people covered must be reduced or the extent to which their nutritional deficits are met must be lowered: that is, breadth, depth, or some combination of the two must be sacrificed.

A basic factor affecting total cost is the number of individuals to be reached. Here, definition of the target group becomes critical because of the arithmetic of population structure. Table 5-2 shows that in one country the target group of 6-month to 6-year-olds plus pregnant and lactating women constitutes 19.0 percent of the population. Lowering the cutoff age to 36 months reduces the group to 9.4 percent. In countries with annual per capita GNP levels of less than $300, less than 35 percent of the population lives in urban areas. Thus, the urban target groups would be about 3 percent of the total population. Applying the income criterion as a nutritional status correlate, it appears that two-thirds of this 3 percent group, or 2 percent of the total population, has a low income. With such targeting, nutrition interventions are perhaps affordable but not inexpensive. Taking into account leakage, the interventions appear to cost between $5 and $15 a year per beneficiary. For India these figures mean an urban target group of about 10 million. Assuming $15 per target-group beneficiary, an annual nutrition budget of $150 million is required, which is only 1.9 percent of the country's GNP. The financial burden of an urban nutrition intervention budget would depend, however, on its size relative to the state and municipal budgets rather than the GNP.

Also important is the possible demand on foreign exchange created by the program. Some interventions such as fortification or nutrient-dense foods might require imports of equipment. Feeding interventions might require food imports, at least during the initial period of building up local agricultural capacity. The pressure these incremental imports place on the balance of payments should be assessed. If the country faces a severe shortage of foreign exchange, projects requiring only a low level of imports become more feasible and attractive. For those projects that do require imports, effort should be made to reduce this dependency over time.

Table 5-2. *Population Structure in West Malaysia*

Population group	Percentage of total population	
	Per age group	*Cumulative*
6 months–1 year	1.70	1.70
1–2 years	3.21	4.91
2–3 years	3.31	8.22
3–4 years	3.21	11.43
4–5 years	3.18	14.61
5–6 years	3.17	17.78
Pregnant women[a]	0.55	18.33
Lactating women[b]	0.66	18.99

Source: Estimates of Population for West Malaysia, 1967 (Kuala Lumpur: Department of Statistics, 1969), cited in "Cereal Fortification: Barriers to Implementation," James Austin and Donald Snodgrass, *Improving the Nutrient Quality of Cereals II* (Washington, D.C.: AID, September 1976), pp. 241–44.
a. Estimated at 75 percent of annual births.
b. Estimated at 50 percent of annual births.

Analysis of Cost Effectiveness

The ideal nutritional intervention achieves maximum benefit at minimum cost. Evaluation systems should generate the information to analyze the project's performance, explain deviations from expected goals, and recommend corrective action. In short, the evaluation is descriptive, diagnostic, and prescriptive. It must be an integral, continuous component of an intervention if it is to provide timely and useful information.

The type of information generated depends on the user of the evaluation data. There are potentially seven principal users.

National policymakers. Politicians formulate national development plans, setting priorities and allocating resources. They are particularly interested in the development benefits from investments in nutrition relative to other sectors. Thus, data relevant to them might include the expected effect on labor productivity (for example, through physical and mental development), deprivation reduction (for example, the percentage of nutritional deficits filled), or income redistribution (for example, numbers of low-income families benefited). They might also be interested in the possible synergies of nutrition with other investments, such as a reduced patient burden on health facilities or a better return on investment in educational infrastructure from the improved mental and cognitive development of well-nourished children.

As governments begin to adopt more holistic development strategies, meeting basic needs (including nutrition) becomes a legitimate goal in itself. Consequently, rates of nutritional improvement would be desired information.

Politicians might also be interested in the numbers, timing, and location of nutrition programs as they relate to high-priority political groups. The need of professional planners and the political leaders for this information is relatively infrequent and tied to planning and election cycles.

Funders. Once program categories have been designated, resources have to be allocated. This money comes primarily from national sources, but international funding has played an important role as well in the relatively recent emergence of nutrition programming.

Funding agencies are interested in accountability for their disbursements. They want to verify that use of their monies conforms to the original intention.

Presumably, funders are also concerned about the desirability of allocating funds to one program rather than others, and so would be interested in performance data. This information should relate to the project goals and to the betterment of the target beneficiaries. The decisions into which such data flow concern the continuance and level of program funding. The more clearly goals are stated, the more likely it is that useful performance information will be generated. Reports to funders should include not only the degree of goal attainment but also explanations of why actual performance deviated from expectations—as it almost always will. Understanding the variance should be the basic diagnostic component of the funding-review process. This approach recognizes the imperfections of nutrition-evaluation techniques, creates a constructive attitude, and may reduce the threatening nature of evaluation. Reports are needed relatively infrequently and are tied to the budgeting cycle.

Sectoral planners. These individuals have been given the responsibility for resources allocated to nutrition activities. Their concern is optimal use of those funds. Unlike national planners, they focus within rather than across sectors. Thus, information needs relate to intervention costs and effects. Their task is not choosing among mutually exclusive alternatives but rather finding the mix of interventions that constitutes an optimal national nutrition program.

They require information on the operational aspects of nutrition programs, especially cost-effectiveness measures. These should be available on a quarterly basis and permit comparison. Many ministries and agencies are likely to be operating the various nutrition programs. Consequently, the sectoral planners' task of interinstitutional coordination and resource allocation is extremely difficult. Standardization of performance indicators will facilitate the job.

Program managers. The individuals operating nutrition projects should be concerned primarily about the efficient and effective delivery of the goods and services to the target group. They need information on how well they are deploying their resources, as revealed, for example, by the cost of delivering the goods or services, coverage of the target group, and the effect on the nutritional problem of that group.

The managers need delivery information quickly and frequently to monitor and adjust their programs' daily operations. Such information serves as an early-warning control mechanism. Data on results are needed less frequently but are important for the managers' periodic review and redesign of the delivery system. The purpose of the evaluation is to provide data that will help the managers do their job more easily, efficiently, and effectively. The evaluation audience is internal, not external. An internal evaluation system ignored by the managers may be symptomatic of irrelevant information, inadequate organizational incentives, or insufficient data analysis, training, or facilities.

Field workers. Internal evaluation data should not be restricted to the manager, since professionals and paraprofessionals can also benefit from evaluation information. They need to know how well they are carrying out their task. This might mean comparing, for example, the number of patients seen or homes visited or meals served during one week with previous periods or with projected performance levels. Data on results such as a reduction in the numbers suffering from third- or second-degree malnutrition can also be provided to emphasize progress. Data requirements can be clearly and narrowly defined.

Such information can serve as a powerful motivating force if it is carefully integrated into a general system of supervision of employees. The motivational value of evaluation data can go even beyond employees in the program.

Beneficiaries. The program beneficiaries have the greatest vested interest in the program's success. The nature of nutritional deficiencies and their alleviation, however, makes benefits less visible than in other problems. Consequently, participation in the program may decline because of insufficient motivation or credibility. Among efforts made to demonstrate results to beneficiaries, growth charts kept by or periodically shown to mothers would be one example of increasing visibility, motivation, and community participation. In fact committees of beneficiaries should provide useful information on both their perceptions and evaluation of the intervention.

Researchers. Nutrition researchers from many disciplines have different perspectives. The evaluation information they seek can be biological, sociological, anthropological, economic, managerial, political, or ethical. The multifaceted etiology of malnutrition elicits such a spectrum. The involvement of academics is important provided that their analyses are of practical rather than purely theoretical value.

Evaluation indicators meeting the needs of these users can be formulated on the basis of outputs, effects, benefits, and costs.[3]

- Outputs are physical results of the intervention's delivery of goods and services, such as coverage of the target group and nutrients delivered.
- Effects are changes in the target group's health and nutritional status resulting from increased use of program outputs.
- Benefits are broader socioeconomic results stemming, in turn, from improved nutrition and health, that is, greater productivity, fewer lost work days, and decreased curative health costs.
- Costs describe the economics of the intervention related to its outputs, effects, and benefits.

Four evaluation indicators can be derived from these elements: operating output, delivery system efficiency, biological cost-effectiveness, and cost-benefit. Within each of these general categories are numerous specific indicators. In all instances the planner should compare results in these categories to intervention goals, explain any variation, and recommend corrective action.

3. This terminology formulation has benefited from the comments and work of Guido J. Deboeck (Rural Operations Review and Support Unit, Agriculture and Rural Development Department, Central Projects Staff, the World Bank). For a highly useful country application of evaluation procedures, see Guido J. Deboeck, "Systems for Monitoring and Evaluation of Nutritional Interventions" (Washington, D.C.: World Bank, Agriculture and Rural Development Department, August 1978).

Indicators of operating output

These measures deal with coverage, nutrients, permanence, personnel, and leakage; they merit the careful attention of program managers and designers who wish to control and improve their operations.

COVERAGE. Examining the effect of the program on the target group to which it is addressed will provide a valuable indicator of the program's success. The coverage of the target group is measured by participation, geographic accessibility, awareness of the program, and the degree to which behavior is changed.

Despite a low and attractive cost-effectiveness ratio, a program may be insignificant because it fails to reach a large portion of the target group. If participation rates are low they must be improved, and their improvement should be monitored. Field-sample interviews will explain the reasons for unsatisfactory participation. For example, target-group mothers should be asked if the distance to clinic or feeding site affects their participation. Because, even if it is accessible, they may be unaware of its services, efforts to disseminate information about the program might be desirable. These efforts should be evaluated according to the behavioral changes they effect within the target group. Evaluations of educational programs are notorious for measuring knowledge or changes in attitude without determining actual changes in behavior and nutritional status.

NUTRIENTS. The percentage of recommended daily allowances delivered and the percentage of deficit covered are useful indicators in determining the program's quantity requirements, and they can provide a tentative check on its probable nutritional significance. For example, severe economic difficulties in one Asian country forced budgetary cuts in the school feeding programs, which reduced the food portion for each child to the point of nutritional insignificance. Measurement and recognition of this fact, in part, led to a higher ration for a more restricted target group.

PERMANENCE. Feeding interventions run the risk of addressing symptoms, not causes. They feed and perhaps rehabilitate children but, as soon as the intervention ends, the children return to their former, insufficient diet. The relapse rate, or the ratio of children who must be brought back to a program divided by total participants, would measure the permanence of the program's effect. Similarly, the number of children whose nutritional status improved initially should be compared with the number whose status remained improved, say, six months after having left the program. The number who remain improved is the relevant figure for evaluation. Programs should be preventive, not just curative; otherwise they simply recycle malnourished children.

A major nutrition program in a South American nation fed a group of children for six months and then switched to another group. Since the children were from 6 to 36 months of age, this feeding might have served as an "inoculation" to get them over their most critical period. Improvement during the feeding period alone was measured, however, so the program's heralded success may not have been permanent.

Another measure of permanence is equalization or improvement in the nutritional status of younger siblings not participating in the intervention. Permanent modification in behavior presumably benefits the younger offspring. If not, was the modification only temporary or applied just to the children in the program?

PERSONNEL. A total figure for lay and professional workers is the first indicator needed for overall manpower planning. Specific figures for lay workers and for professionals indicate how labor intensive or skill intensive the operation is. The more labor intensive a project, the greater its supervisory and organizational demands, but such a program may be attractive specifically because it creates jobs. The more skill intensive, the greater pressure the program places on scarce professional resources.

LEAKAGE. The commodity can be diverted from the target group at many stages in a food-delivery intervention. This leakage can reduce the program's effectiveness and increase its delivery costs. Unless leakages are documented, the quantity of nutrients to put into the delivery system to ensure that the needed amounts reach the target group cannot be determined.

Transport and storage loss and the resale of delivered goods occur because of faulty logistics and control systems. Loss of nutrients through consumption by family members outside the target group or because of bulk constraint is related to the type of diet and to cultural feeding patterns. Resale and unauthorized consumption, as well as substitution of the nutrient for existing food, constitute leakages related to the family's economic situation. Finally, absorption loss is the result of problems such as diarrheal disease and inadequate absorptive capacity. Consumption by other members of the target family is clearly not a societal loss, but it either reduces the desired effect on the target group or increases the cost of achieving that effect.

Although these leakages are difficult to document, they are critical control points for program managers, and they can significantly affect intervention economics. The information system should, through sampling, verify the nutrient flow as a means of estimating leakage. Shipping and inventory records can document transport and storage loss. Calculation of nutrients delivered compared to actual consumption, as measured by dietary survey, can provide an estimate of diversion to nontarget groups. The substitution effect can be quantified by comparing consumption before and after supplementation relative to the size of the ration.

Indicators of efficiency

These indicators reveal how efficiently the delivery system is supplying the target group with needed nutrients. Delivery is an essential though insufficient prerequisite to achieving a biological effect. A manager can therefore use this measure, in the absence of specific measurements of health status, as a general indicator of the likelihood of the biological effect.

DOLLARS PER TARGET-GROUP RECIPIENT. The calculation can be started by dividing the total cost of providing nutrition education, delivering food or seeds, and the like, by the number of persons actually receiving the goods or services. Because the cost of reaching the target group member is of greater concern, and because not all recipients will be target group members, the difference between "dollars per target group recipient" and "dollars per total recipients" will represent the cost of overcoverage. This "wastage" can be traded off against incremental expenditures necessary to reduce the costs of overcoverage by focusing more accurately on the target.

DOLLARS PER NUTRIENT-DEFICIT REDUCTION. Interventions are intended to reduce nutritional deficits. This measure is computed by dividing total cost by the preintervention nutrient deficit minus the nutrients delivered (food consumption change converted through standard tables to nutrient equivalents). All direct nutrition interventions attempt to increase nutrient consumption, whether through direct feeding, fortification, nutrition education, or subsidized consumption. A difficulty arises in comparing alternative interventions using this indicator. When several nutrients are delivered, costs cannot readily be allocated among them. Therefore, comparisons of the cost of multiple- and single-nutrient interventions are not easy. Nonetheless, this indicator can be used effectively to judge a single intervention against its original goals.

Indicators of biological cost effectiveness

Planners and funders are particularly interested in bio-indicators. The basic measurement is the ratio between costs and the percentage change in nutritional or health status, measured from standard longitudinal or cross-sectional data. The possible indicators are (a) dollars per infant mortality rate change; (b) dollars per 1–3-year mortality rate change; (c) dollars per morbidity change; and (d) dollars per degree malnutrition change (anthropometry).

Infant mortality rates can be monitored readily, but underreporting is likely in retrospective data, especially those derived from census statistics. Preschooler mortality data are more reliable. Mortality, however, is the extreme consequence of malnutrition and of much lower incidence than general malnutrition. A small evaluation sample can render this measure statistically insignificant. Information on morbidity is especially desirable in distinguishing its effect on mortality from that of malnutrition.[4]

This is probably the most difficult measure about which to get uniform and reliable data. Anthropometry is more reliable and measures changes in malnutrition's severity reasonably well; it is

4. Lincoln C. Chen, "Control of Diarrheal Disease, Morbidity, and Mortality: Some Strategic Issues" (position paper for the National Academy of Sciences Symposium on Effective Interventions to Reduce Infection in Malnourished Populations, Port-au-Prince, Haiti, June 12–16, 1977) (Washington, D.C.: National Academy of Sciences, Food and Nutrition Board, 1977); reprinted in *American Journal of Clinical Nutrition*, vol. 31 (November-December 1978), pp. 2284–91.

the principal indicator of biological change. For a full picture, these indicators should be used in combination rather than singly.

Changes in all bio-indicators occur slowly. Some interventions such as nutrition education can be expected to take effect over a longer period. Accordingly, comparisons of the cost effectiveness of a program should span several years and measure cumulative costs and benefits. Simple annual comparisons should be viewed only as partial pictures suggesting tentative judgments. Judged against a spacious time horizon, programs with the greatest effect at the lowest cost over the shortest time are preferable.

Indicators of cost-benefit ratio

Cost-benefit analysis allows comparison of nutrition and non-nutrition investments; it is particularly useful to planners facing the task of setting investment priorities. But this method is difficult to apply to nutrition programs because of the difficulties in measuring effects and quantifying social benefits in economic terms. Nonetheless, approximation of benefits is possible and preferable to qualitative statements.

A reduction in mortality generates a value to society equivalent to the discounted value of the future production of each individual saved. Some would argue that only the net benefit—the individual's production less consumption—should be used, that is, net resource savings.[5] Production can be valued at the minimum wage times the average working life reduced by the average unemployment rate. Although the functional relation between malnutrition and future productivity has not been clearly established, mental and physical retardation are thought to lower the quality of human capital. A factor measuring improvement in productivity may be estimated and applied to the discounted stream of minimum wages earned during an average work life to calculate the program's incremental economic benefit.[6]

Where the intervention is directed at adult workers, productivity

5. For a further discussion of the valuation issue, see Robert J. Saunders and Jeremy J. Warford, *Village Water Supply* (Baltimore: Johns Hopkins University Press, 1976), and Victor Fuchs, *Who Shall Live?* (New York: Basic Books, 1974).

6. Marcelo Selowsky and Lance Taylor, "The Economics of Malnourished Children: An Example of Disinvestment in Human Capital," *Economic Development and Cultural Change*, vol. 22, no. 1 (October 1973), pp. 17–30.

gains can be measured and valued directly as the worth of the additional work they perform.[7] Increased productivity may, however, increase parents' consumption without necessarily resulting in improvement for children in their families. If the intervention improves adult health, sick days saved, in which work is found that does not displace others, represent increased income for the beneficiary and output for the nation. To the extent that intervention prevents sickness for which the target group would have to underwrite the treatment, the beneficiaries have realized a savings. Their total expenditure on private health care can be calculated and a percentage of savings computed, based on estimated program results. Existing health-care facilities may then be able to attend to more or needier individuals.

Some interventions—such as the development of nutrient-dense foods from underutilized food sources or the improvement of food marketing, storage, and handling—can cut wastage and can increase food resources. Better nutrition may improve cognitive development and result in better school performance—that is, fewer failures and more efficient learning behavior. This development would doubtless enhance the value of the country's educational investment, but empirical data to quantify this benefit do not exist.

7. See, for example, Samir S. Basta and Anthony Churchill, "Iron Deficiency and the Productivity of Adult Males in Indonesia," World Bank Staff Working Paper, no. 175 (Washington, D.C.: World Bank, 1974).

6

●−●‥●−●

Program Management

The design and selection of interventions should embody explicit
consideration of their managerial needs to avoid jeopardizing their
implementation by mismanagement. The evaluation system considered above provides for an exchange of information and thus
serves as a link between planners and managers. Program management should, however, be viewed more broadly as the art and science of directing resources and activities toward specific objectives,
and, as such, managerial considerations are relevant to both national policy and program operation. It is therefore important to highlight several dimensions of program management that were al-
luded to in previous chapters and to outline possible barriers to
implementation.

Implementation by national or municipal organizations can
founder on managerial weakness at the operating level. Each intervention, because of its distinctive characteristics and its unique operating environment, presents different managerial problems
and faces different constraints. Nonetheless, each intervention
plan should be scrutinized at least for the following.

Control

The control function ensures that program activities proceed according to plan. It demands a monitoring system to warn the man-

1. Consideration of the managerial activities should recognize that managerial
processes and techniques must be adapted to the sociocultural and institutional conditions prevailing in the country. See, for example, Jon R. Moris, "The Transfer-
ability of Western Management Tradition into the Public Service Sectors: An East
African Perspective" (paper for the Bellagio Conference on Public Management
Education and Training, August 11–15, 1976).

ager of deviations requiring corrective action. The manager should identify and control those activities within the delivery operation which most critically affect the success of the intervention. Control requires timely and selective information. Excessively long reports burden the manager and stifle efforts at control. Records of the numbers fed daily, or attendance at clinics or nutrition education sessions, or of quantities of food delivered, fortified, or sold can serve as simple control indicators when they are compared with previous days or to general program targets. The evaluation system considered in the previous chapter is an essential part of a management control system.

Personnel

The scarcest resources in some developing countries are professional management and technical personnel. Consequently, an intervention designer must assess professional manpower needs and compare them with available resources. Management positions in nutrition programs are frequently allocated low salaries; consequently, such programs do not attract the best people, and program implementation suffers. Good managers will figuratively pay their own way in improved program performance.

Nonetheless, scarce funding dictates all possible economy in personnel. Because many tasks need not employ expensive and scarce medical professionals, for example, a fruitful avenue to pursue is the use of paraprofessionals. The manager should analyze tasks, assess their skill requirements, and match their needs with people available. Efforts should also be made to recruit and train local community members; this will minimize costs and increase that community participation which is critical to the effectiveness of the program. Care, however, should be taken not to overburden community workers who need continual training to update and expand their skills, as well as adequate supervisory and support services.

Publicity and Delivery

These activities correspond to the marketing function. The first task for the manager is to understand the characteristics, problems, and behavior of the target group. This analysis of the clientele is necessary to locate, motivate, and reach the beneficiaries. The goods or services and the delivery mechanism should be engineered according to the specifications of site location, delivery timing, product form, and information dissemination. Active involvement of the community in the assessment of needs and the design of interventions is critical in this regard.

The management of information can be important in reaching the target group. Often the most nutritionally needy are the least accessible and the least aware of program services. Publicity through radio, bulletins, word of mouth, and home visits may be in order. Too often program facilities are underused because of insufficient marketing. Most of the urban environment and economic behavior information in chapter 3 is relevant to this task.

Finances

The manager will generally operate under severe financial constraints. Accordingly, care should be taken to manage funds as efficiently as possible. Simple project budgets should be employed, and the monitoring system should provide cost data to allow periodic actual-to-budget comparisons. Analysis of variance will help managers improve their use of funds.

The manager should consider means of increasing project resources. Community contributions may be a source that will be more forthcoming if the program meets a clearly perceived need and the community is heavily committed to its aims. Again, the critical importance of community involvement in program design and implementation is apparent.

Organization

The foregoing management functions cannot be effectively performed outside an appropriate organizational structure. Many organizational forms are possible, but in all cases the manager should delineate precise tasks and assign clear responsibilities to carry them out. The manager should match the responsibilities assigned with authority to carry them out.

Planning from the top down frequently falters in the face of community apathy or resistance. This problem arises from the misfit with community needs that the vertical approach often creates.

Intervention design should begin with the beneficiaries—and so should intervention implementation. The involvement of beneficiaries in diagnosing the problem, delivering goods or services, and controlling program performance should be a basic objective of intervention organization. In effect, what is required is a "bottom-up"–"top-down" approach to the planning and implementation of nutrition programs.

At the national level, one general organizational issue exists. The various direct and indirect interventions—nutrition, health, water systems, agriculture, education—traditionally have been the responsibility of different ministries or departments with little experience in coordinating their activities. Administrative systems are structured vertically within sectors. Total integration of nutrition programs requires horizontal organizational structures. Unless coordinating mechanisms are developed, field personnel can be confused by multiple or even conflicting supervision—and programs doomed to failure.

Several measures can be taken. First, strong support for integrated nutrition programming should be clearly communicated from the highest political levels. Second, an executive committee can develop a plan in which joint objectives are formulated, institutional roles and responsibilities are delineated, and commitment is elicited. This committee can become the motivating force facilitating horizontal coordination of relatively autonomous and equally powerful ministries. The committee must be headed by a strong leader adept at managing institutional relations. Third, a technical supporting staff, perhaps from the national planning department, can monitor the operation and resolve technical problems special to coordination. Fourth, the coordinating committee should be given a special budget to cover selected activities essential to the various organizations and shared by them, such as training, educational materials development, personnel, and logistics. Budgetary power will invest the coordinating body with indisputable authority. An integrated, multi-intervention approach offers considerable potential and should be pursued, but it is a demanding task requiring managerial expertise, broad institutional support, and strong political backing. A coordinating committee without institutional instruments of leverage will be ineffectual.

It should be noted that, in dealing with selected urban areas, municipal organizational structure may be more critical than the national one. Nonetheless, similar issues exist. Municipal departments handle specific social services in vertical structures that parallel the national structure. The planning and coordinating approach suggested is also applicable to the specific urban setting.

Barriers to Implementation

The implementation and management of nutrition interventions generally face barriers from operational and political factors. The task of the nutrition planner is therefore to identify constraints on feasibility and attempt to circumvent or modify them through designs that narrow the gap between the feasible and the desirable. Because the redesign effort is a continuous, iterative process, the concept of barriers can be useful in the process of intervention design and selection by providing perspective and by focusing attention on critical factors. Although the surmountability of barriers varies, potential barriers can be generalized into four categories: as they relate to the distribution system, to the product delivered, to nutrient intake, and to institutional and political factors. The following checklist can assist the planner in analyzing the barriers to a successful intervention.

Distribution system
- Transport: Are adequate transport services and infrastructure available to transport the food to the target group or the target group to the food distribution point?
- Outlet coverage: Are the food-distribution outlets sufficiently numerous and properly located to reach most of the target group, especially the most severely deficient?
- Storage and handling: Do storage facilities have adequate capacity and quality to handle efficiently the programmed volume of food?
- Pilferage: Does a control system minimize the risk of pilferage?

Product delivered
- Technology: Can the food-processing technology, equipment, and materials provide the product with the desired nutrient characteristics?
- Supply: Is the domestic supply of the foods adequate to provide the quantity and quality of needed nutrients?
- Packaging: Are adequate packaging materials available at acceptable prices?

Nutrient intake

- Organoleptic characteristics: Have consumer-acceptability tests been carried out to test the suitability of the products' tastes, textures, sights, smells, and cooking properties?
- Food habits: Will the way food is prepared, served, or shared among family members significantly reduce nutrient intake of the delivered food of the target group?
- Substitution: Why and to what extent will the intervention simply replace existing food expenditures?
- Consumption by nontarget family: Of the intervention characteristics that permit leakages to nontarget families, which are most significant and most amenable to correction?
- Price: How much will the target group have to pay for the intervention and how will price affect intake?

Institutional and political factors

- Organization: Does the implementing institution have the necessary organizational and managerial resources to carry out the intervention?
- Institutional relations: Do coordinating mechanisms exist to ensure effective cooperation between institutions in planning, communications, and implementation?
- Political: What effect will the intervention have on political power groups?

Table 6-1 provides tentative judgments about the height of barriers to a successful intervention. Although the matrix contains judgments about the distribution system, the product itself, and nutrient intake, it omits judgments about institutional and political barriers, since they are too site specific for generalization. It must be emphasized nevertheless that institutional barriers frequently arise. Since they address problems with wide implications, nutrition interventions often cut across the health, public sanitation, agriculture, and education sectors, where institutional rivalry and traditional specialization often throw up formidable barriers to cooperation and coordination between institutions. As for political barriers, it should first be recognized that the fundamental prerequisite to a successful intervention is the government's will to confront the malnutrition problem. In the absence of this commitment, nutrition programming is futile. At best, intervention will be tokenism; at worst, an insidious palliative.

Table 6-1. *Matrix of Barriers to Urban Intervention*

	Fortification		On-site feeding		Take-home feeding		Government ration shop[a]		Commercial channel		
Location of barrier	Micro-nutrient	Macro-nutrient	Tradi-tional foods	New nutri-tional foods	Tradi-tional foods	New nutri-tional foods	With means test	With-out means test	Food stamp	General price subsidy	Income transfer
Distribution system											
Transport availability	L	L	M	M	L	L	M	M	L	L	L
Outlet coverage	L	L	M	M	L	L	M	M	L	L	L
Storage and handling losses	L	L	M	M	L	L	L	L	L	L	L
Pilferage losses	L	L	M	M	L	L	M	M	L	L	L
Managerial skills	L	L	M	M	L	L	M	L	H	L	H
Product											
Technological requirements	L	L	L	M	L	M	L	L	L	L	L
Raw material availability	L	L	L	M	L	M	L	L	L	L	L
Packaging	L	L	L	L	L	M	L	L	L	L	L
Nutritional value	L	L	M	L	M	L	M	M	M	M	M
Nutrient intake											
Organoleptic characteristics	L	L	L	H	L	H	L	L	L	L	L
Food beliefs	L	M	L	M	L	H	L	H	L	L	L
Intrafamilial distribution	H	H	H	L	H	H	H	H	H	H	H
Substitution	L	L	L	M	M	M	M	M	M	L	L
Reselling	L	L	L	L	M	M	M	M	M	L	L
Changed expenditure pattern	H	L	L	L	M	L	M	M	M	H	H
Nontarget-family consumption	H	H	L	L	M	L	M	M	M	H	H
Price	L	M	M	M	M	M	L	L	L	L	L

Note: L=low, M=medium, H=high barrier.
a. Assumes traditional staple distributed.

7

•••

A Concluding Note

Urban malnutrition is an acute dimension of urban poverty with a particularly wasting effect on a nation's human capital. Malnutrition can be defeated only by a larger socioeconomic attack on underdevelopment and distributional inequities. Given a general commitment to these goals, nutrition interventions are valuable because they accelerate the conquest of malnutrition.

This study has presented an approach to nutrition programming in urban areas. The first step in programming is to diagnose the nutritional problem according to the type, severity, causes, and victims of nutritional deficiencies. Diagnosis of the problem and design of the subsequent intervention must be founded on a solid information base. The three categories of information identified as requiring examination are urban environment, economic behavior, and nutritional status. Consideration of these categories identified the most useful data and means of their collection. A guiding tenet of information collection is "be selective," by collecting as few data as are needed for reasonable diagnosis and design.

Nine types of direct nutrition intervention—nutrition education, on-site feeding, take-home feeding, nutrient-dense foods, ration shops, food coupon programs, fortification, direct nutrient dosage, and food processing and distribution—were analyzed. The integration of indirect interventions—health, water and sanitation, family planning—with the direct interventions was also examined to highlight the desirability of a holistic approach to nutrition programming. Despite the scarcity of empirical data on relative program performance, critical design variables were delineated and judgments were made about optimal intervention design.

To facilitate the task of selecting among interventions, financial analysis and evaluation methods were presented. Alternative methodological approaches are possible, but those presented have considerable potential for producing significant and readily usable data. Finally, a brief discussion of intervention management stressed the critical importance of managerial components essential to the effective implementation of the nutrition program.

As the year 2000 approaches, the probable quadrupling of the urban population in the developing world by that year seems almost overwhelming. The specter of even more severe urban malnutrition looms on the horizon. Firm political commitment to meeting basic needs and eradicating malnutrition is an essential prerequisite to effective action. Explicit policies and goals, systematic planning, careful intervention design, professional management, and true community involvement are the critical ingredients of the alchemy that can transform political will into improved well-being of the urban poor. It is hoped that the guidelines presented here will assist planners to accomplish more efficiently and effectively the major task of confronting urban malnutrition.

APPENDIX

.•••

Micronutrient Deficiencies

Because of the high prevalence of micronutrient deficiencies and their individual significance as a public health problem, these deficiencies merit examination in some detail.

Vitamin A

Vitamin A deficiency is one of the most common deficiency diseases in the world and is a known cause of preventable blindness.[1] Its occurrence has been reported in Burma, Sri Lanka, Bangladesh, India, Philippines, Viet Nam, South Korea, and Thailand.[2] Xerophthalmia, one of the stages of the deficiency,[3] is seen frequently in Middle East and African countries, including Iran, Iraq, Jordan, Lebanon, Libya, Sudan, Tanzania, and Egypt. In the Americas, epidemics have been reported in Haiti, El Salvador, and Brazil.

An inadequate vitamin A intake is the most common cause of the deficiency. The deficiency is a problem only in areas where B-carotene is the main dietary source of vitamin A; and is rare in countries where 50 percent of the source is preformed vitamin A.[4]

Note: My coauthors for this section in the original report to the World Bank were: Barbara Millen Posner, Eileen Kennedy, Flavio Valente, and Stanley Gershoff.

1. S. G. Srikantia, "Human Vitamin A Requirements," *World Review of Nutrition and Dietetics*, no. 20 (1975), pp. 184–230.

2. Ibid.

3. Beverly Winikoff, "Vitamin A," in *Priorities in Child Nutrition,* vol. 3 (Cambridge, Mass.: Harvard University, School of Public Health, 1975), pp. 234–35.

4. Srikantia, "Human Vitamin A Requirements."

Factors other than intake may predispose a child to the deficiency.[5] Newborn infants whose mothers have had prolonged low intake start life with hepatic vitamin A deficits. If breastfeeding is discontinued (as trends in urban areas in developing countries seem to indicate), vitamin A requirements may not be met. This is particularly true if vegetable-based weaning foods (low in preformed vitamin A) are introduced. Studies in India indicate that intakes of preschool children are 40 percent below requirements, since the majority of vitamin A is derived from B-carotene.

In Asia deficiency signs occur in from 30 to 50 percent of children according to studies in Indonesia, Thailand, and India.[6] Frequently, the disease is associated with protein-calorie malnutrition (PCM) but with varying degrees of prevalence in the malnourished populations. In Indonesia, for example, 75 percent of the children with PCM have vitamin A deficiency, whereas only 10 percent of those with PCM in Brazil are similarly affected.[7] In Latin America clinical signs of vitamin A deficiency were seen in from 40 to 60 percent of children hospitalized with marasmus and kwashiorkor, whereas in India only 14 of 1,565 cases with PCM had vitamin A deficiency.[8]

Because protein and vitamin A deficiencies frequently occur together, scientists have attempted to determine their relation. Some have suggested that vitamin A deficiency decreases the use of ingested proteins, thereby enhancing protein deficiency. Others have suggested that the body stores of vitamin A may not be available to the host with PCM because of inadequate mechanisms for protein

5. P. S. Venkatachalam and C. Gopolan, "Kwashiorkor in Hyderabad and Coonoor," *Indian Journal of Medical Research*, vol. 48 (1960), pp. 645–53; N. Pralhad Rao, Darshan Singh, and M. C. Swaminathan, "Nutrition Status of Preschool Children of Rural Communities near Hyderabad," *Indian Journal of Medical Research*, vol. 57 (1969), p. 2132.

6. Aroon Netrasiri and Cherdchalong Netrasiri, "Kwashiorkor in Bangkok, An Analytic Study of Fifty-four Cases," *Journal of Tropical Pediatrics* (1955), pp. 148–55; S. M. Pereira and S. J. Baker, "Hematologic Studies in Kwashiorkor," *American Journal of Clinical Nutrition*, vol. 18 (1966), pp. 413–20; and Ousa Thanangkul, J. Anne Whitaker, and Eleanor G. Fort, "Malnutrition in Northern Thailand," *American Journal of Clinical Nutrition*, vol. 18 (1966), pp. 379–89.

7. M. Batista, "Consideraçãoes sôbre o Problema da Vitimina A no Nordeste Brasileiro," *O Hospital*, vol. 75, no. 3 (March 1969), cited in Winikoff, "Vitamin A," p. 236.

8. Winikoff, "Vitamin A," pp. 236–37.

Table A-1. *Percentage Distribution of Low-income Families in Rio de Janeiro by Level of Nutritional Adequacy and Income*

Nutrient (percentage of requirement)	Lowest income level	Second-lowest income level
Calories		
20–60	7.2	2.7
60–99	54.2	26.0
100	38.5	71.3
Protein		
20–60	4.2	0.9
60–99	18.1	10.1
100	77.7	84.1
Iron		
20–60	13.3	3.3
60–99	49.4	28.5
100	37.3	68.2
Vitamin A		
20	17.5	4.9
20–40	23.5	9.4
40–60	12.7	12.2
60–80	10.8	14.4
80–100	9.6	13.3
100–150	26.0	45.8

Source: The Getúlio Vargas Foundation, Brazilian Institute of Economics, *Pesquisa sôbre Consumo Alimentar* (Rio de Janeiro: Praia de Botafogo 190, 1973), pp. 136–95. Used by permission of the Foundation.

transport. Neither of these theories suggests a cause-effect relation between the nutrients. Vitamin A deficiency is invariably associated with protein deficiency, although the converse is not true. This latter fact supports the thesis that vitamin A deficits should be evaluated independently of calorie evaluations of dietary adequacy.

Although the refeeding of marginally nourished children increases growth and their requirement for vitamin A, failure to provide vitamin A can precipitate severe deficiency signs.

In a Rio de Janeiro study, caloric intake was not the most limiting factor in the diet. From Table A-1 it can be seen that vitamin A was the most limiting nutrient in both income groups.[9]

9. The Getúlio Vargas Foundation, *Pesquisa sôbre Consumo Alimentar* (Rio de Janeiro, 1973), pp. 136–95.

Table A-2. *Summary of Major Clinical and Biochemical Findings in Adult Women in West Pakistan*
(percentage of prevalence)

	Pregnant and lactating		Nonpregnant, nonlactating	
Finding	Urban	Rural	Urban	Rural
Clinical goiter	11.89	4.48	6.12	3.61
Low plasma albumin	66.7	37.5	12.5	42.8
Low hemoglobin	100.0	92.0	53.6	26.3
Low plasma vitamin A	0	70.0	0	25.0
Low serum vitamin C	15.3	28.5	17.8	11.7
Bitot's spot	3.26	3.49	3.95	7.03
Angular lesions	3.26	—	3.27	0.92
Swollen red papillae	5.30	4.89	5.85	3.06
Pallor	73.0	83.9	51.15	56.57

Source: The Directorate of Nutrition Survey and Research, *Nutrition Survey of West Pakistan* (Islamabad: Ministry of Health, Labour, and Family Planning, June 1970), pp. 142–43.

A survey conducted in São Paulo also shows clearly that caloric intake is not the most limiting factor in the diet.[10] The diets were always more deficient in such other nutrients as iron, riboflavin, niacin, and calcium. This deficit could be explained by the fact that the diet is low in foods of animal origin, which are the best sources of such nutrients. Even when caloric intake was adequate, significant deficiencies of other nutrients were still observed. Vitamin A deficiency was widespread. Some 34 percent of the population appraised for vitamin A status had deficient levels of vitamin A. The most vulnerable groups were the pregnant and lactating women, 90 percent of whom had deficient or low blood levels of vitamin A.

A Pakistan study of rural and urban persons supports belief in the wide prevalence of specific nutrient deficiencies.[11] Table A-2 outlines the major clinical findings in the comparison of pregnant with nonpregnant urban and rural women. The urban pregnant women had a higher incidence of clinical goiter, a lower plasma

10. Escola Paulista de Medicina, Instituto de Medicina Preventiva, Universidade de São Paulo, Instituto de Pesquisas Econômicas, *Estado Nutricional de Crianças de 6 à 60 Mêses no Município de São Paulo,* vol. 2, *Análise de Datos* (São Paulo: Minestério de Educação e Cultura, 1975), pp. 49–62.

11. The Directorate of Nutrition Survey and Research, *Nutrition Survey of West Pakistan* (Islamabad: Ministry of Health, Labour, and Family Planning, June 1970), pp. 142–43.

albumin, and lower hemoglobin than their rural counterparts. Seventy percent of the rural pregnant women had low plasma vitamin A as opposed to zero percent of the urban pregnant women.

Anemia

Children with kwashiorkor are frequently found to have moderate anemia, which has been described as orthochronic normocytic[12] and is from protein deficiency alone.[13] Reports from South Africa, Egypt, Uganda, Indonesia, and South America show, however, that a fair percentage of children with PCM have megaloblastic macrocytic anemia secondary to deficiency.[14] Intestinal absorption appears unchanged in PCM, so it can only be speculated as to the possible dietary and altered folate metabolism causes of the deficiency. A high prevalence of folate and iron deficiency in women of childbearing age was found in Kiryat Shomoneh, a community in upper Galilee.[15] Below normal blood folate levels seen in 47 percent of mothers and 53.4 percent of children were supported by dietary studies. Although caloric intakes were deficient in only 30 percent of the individuals studied, all individual diets were deficient in folate; 60 percent of women's and children's diets were below requirements of iron. Serum iron levels were below normal in 59 percent and 41 percent of women and children, respectively. Protein intake was adequate in most cases. Calorie deficits existed, but micronutrient deficits in folate, iron, and ascorbic acid were even more striking. The authors of the study proposed three factors as causes of iron and folate deficiencies: increased demands of pregnancy, rapid growth in infancy and childhood, and dietary intake. Twenty-four-hour recall, however, tends to underestimate average micronutrient intake over a prolonged period because foods with vitamins and minerals are generally consumed less regularly than those providing principally calories and proteins.

12. M. K. Sandozai and others, "Kwashiorkor, A Clinico-haematological study," *British Medical Journal*, vol. 2 (1963), pp. 93–96.

13. Charles H. Halsted and others, "Anemia of Kwashiorkor in Cairo: Deficiencies of Protein, Iron, and Folic Acid," *American Journal of Clinical Nutrition*, vol. 22 (1969), pp. 1371–81.

14. S. M. Pereira and Almos Begum, "The Manifestations and Management of Severe Protein-Calorie Malnutrition (Kwashiorkor)," *World Review of Nutrition and Dietetics*, vol. 19 (1970), pp. 1–50.

15. S. Levy and others, "Nutritional Survey in an Iron- and Folate-Deficient Population," *American Journal of Clinical Nutrition*, vol. 28 (1975), pp. 1454–57.

The occurrence in a significant number of children of megaloblastic anemia with or without kwashiorkor should not overshadow the fact that iron deficiency may coexist with, and in many areas of the world is, the most commonly encountered anemia in childhood malnutrition.[16] In several areas in South America and the Caribbean, more than 30 percent of the children under 1 year had hemoglobins of 10 grams per 100 milliliters.[17]

In women of childbearing age, losses secondary to menses, depletion during pregnancy, prolonged lactation, and inadequate dietary intake precipitate the deficiency. In India three-fourths or more of the women are estimated to have iron deficiency anemia. In Venezuela 57.9 percent of the pregnant women were found to have hemoglobins under 12 grams per 100 milliliters, and in Trinidad 31.1 percent had hemoglobins under 10 grams per 100 milliliters. For nonpregnant women, percentages in these categories were 18.9 percent and 3.5 percent, respectively.[18]

The profile of dietary nutrients assessed by two-day food records among Ethiopian women, privileged and nonprivileged, suggests calories were not most limiting. The strikingly high intake of iron is the result of consumption of the cereal teff, which contributed to the rarity of iron deficiency anemia in the highland Ethiopian women. General dietary inadequacies led to retardation of intrauterine growth, estimated from birth weights of children.[19]

Although women and children, particularly male children, have been determined as target groups, adult males in some populations have inadequate hemoglobin levels.[20] Basta found 45 percent of Indonesian workers in a rubber plant to have anemia (percentage of hemoglobin under 11 grams).[21] A Venezuelan survey found 41.7 percent of men tested had low hemoglobins, 14 percent with

16. Pereira and Begum, "Kwashiorkor," p. 50.

17. Yaro R. Gandra, "La anemia ferropenia en la población de América Latina y el Caribe," *Boletín de la Oficina Sanitaria Panamericana* (May 1970), p. 382.

18. Ibid., p. 378.

19. Mehari Gebre-Medhin and Afeba Gobezie, "Dietary Intake in the Third Trimester of Pregnancy and Birth Weight of Offspring among Nonprivileged and Privileged Women," *American Journal of Clinical Nutrition*, vol. 28 (1975), pp. 1322–29.

20. David Burman, "Hemoglobin Levels in Normal Infants Aged 3 to 24 Months and the Effect of Iron," *Archives of Disease in Childhood*, vol. 47 (1972), p. 261.

21. Samir S. Basta, "Iron Deficiency Anemia in Adult Males and Work Capacity," (Ph.D. dissertation, Massachusetts Institute of Technology, Department of Nutrition and Food Science, Cambridge, Mass., December 1973).

less than 12 grams per 100 milliliters. Significant correlations were found between anemia, worker output, and morbidity.

Goiter

Simple goiter is a unique public health problem in that its prophylaxis is well established, easy to administer, and relatively inexpensive. It is present in demarcated areas of the world, and where it occurs it is widespread. It is, however, rare in urban areas. Its presence may be no more than a minor inconvenience to those most directly affected, but the results in children can be devastating.[22] Although the incidence of defects in children born to goitrous mothers varies considerably, a certain percentage of them are born deaf or mentally and motor retarded as well (cretinism). It may be that viral and bacterial agents or inborn errors of metabolism may be to blame rather than iodine deficiency. Where the goiter rate rises above 50 percent, mental defectives and deaf mutes may constitute 4 percent or more of the population.[23] But this relationship is not well enough documented to be conclusive.

Dietary deficiencies not necessarily seen in conjunction with caloric deficiency are the most common cause of the deficit. Deficiency can also be caused by goitrogenic agents in the diet that render iodine unavailable. Contamination of water supplies with waterborne goitrogens or staple foods with known goitrogenic properties, such as cassava, may precipitate the condition.[24] Deficient circulating levels of hormones containing iodine cause overstimulation and enlargement of the thyroid.

Vitamin C (Ascorbic Acid)

Evaluation of thirty-three nutrition surveys by the U.S. Interdepartmental Committee on Nutrition and National Defense found

22. Beverly Winikoff, "Endemic Goiter," in *Priorities in Child Nutrition,* vol. 3, pp. 246–53.

23. M. Stott and others, "The Distribution and Cause of Endemic Goitre in the United Provinces," *Indian Journal of Medical Research,* vol. 20 (1932), p. 139.

24. E. Gaitán, "Waterborne Goitrogens and Their Role in the Etiology of Endemic Goiter," *World Review of Nutrition and Dietetics,* vol. 17 (1973), pp. 53–90.

that, in twenty countries between 1956 and 1967, frank scurvy was rare. Some 5 percent of the population in two-thirds of the countries was, however, classified as having low serum ascorbic acid.

Vitamin D

In developing countries of the tropics and subtropics, vitamin D deficiency occurs in a variable proportion of young infants and children. Nutrition surveys in Viet Nam, India, Israel, Egypt, Nigeria, and South Africa indicate the clinical prevalence of the deficiency in from 0.1 percent to 20 percent of infants and young children.[25] In a recent WHO survey in North Africa, from 45 to 60 percent of the children examined showed signs of rickets.[26] Mainly affected were children aged 3 to 18 months, especially in urban areas. Causes of the deficiency are dietary vitamin D inadequacy, poor housing, and social customs that prevent exposure of the child's skin to sunlight.

The problem of vitamin D deficiency seems to be overshadowed by the prevalence of PCM. The latter, by retarding growth, checks the appearance of rachitic deformities that occur most readily in growing bones.

Thiamin

Despite tremendous advances in reducing beriberi, this disease still needs the attention of public health professionals. Even in Japan, a recent report concluded that 10 percent of the population still had symptoms suggesting thiamin deficiency.[27] In Burma and Thailand extension of rice mills into rural areas seems to stimulate a rise in beriberi, although systematic studies have not yet confirmed this development.[28]

25. Joint FAO/WHO Expert Committee on Nutrition, *Requirements of Ascorbic Acid, Vitamin D, B12', Folate and Iron,* WHO Technical Report Series no. 452 (Geneva, 1970), pp. 1–75.

26. Joint FAO/WHO Expert Committee on Nutrition, *Seventh Report,* WHO Technical Report Series no. 377 (Geneva, 1967), pp. 1–84.

27. Wallace F. Aykroyd, *Conquest of Deficiency Diseases,* WHO Basic Studies no. 24 (Geneva, 1970), p. 26.

28. "Nutrition: A Review of the WHO Programme-I," *WHO Chronicle,* vol. 26, no. 4 (April 1972), pp. 160–80.

In summary, deficiency diseases that deserve the highest global priority according to WHO are (a) PCM, because of its high mortality rate, its wide prevalence, and the irreversible physical and sometimes mental damage it may cause; (b) xerophthalmia, because of its contribution to the mortality of malnourished children, its relatively wide prevalence, and the permanent blindness it causes; (c) nutritional anemias, because of their wide distribution, their contribution to mortality from many other conditions, and their effects on working capacity; and (d) endemic goiter, because of its wide distribution. In some more limited areas of the world other nutritional problems such as beriberi, pellagra, and rickets may also warrant a high priority.

The full range of World Bank publications, both free and for sale, is described in the *Catalog of World Bank Publications*, and of the continuing research program of the World Bank, in *World Bank Research Program: Abstracts of Current Studies*. The most recent edition of each is available without charge from:

PUBLICATIONS UNIT
THE WORLD BANK
1818 H STREET, N.W.
WASHINGTON, D.C. 20433
U.S.A.

DATE DUE

MAY 1 3 2003		
DEC 0 8 2003		
JAN 1 5 2013		
MAY 0 5 2013		

Demco, Inc. 38-293

DEMCO